FLYING
SOLO

ALSO BY LEONARD KRIEGEL

Falling into Life

Quitting Time

On Men and Manhood

Notes for the Two-Dollar Window

Working Through

Edmund Wilson

The Long Walk Home

FLYING
SOLO

REIMAGINING
MANHOOD,
COURAGE,
AND LOSS

LEONARD KRIEGEL

BEACON PRESS
BOSTON

BEACON PRESS
25 Beacon Street
Boston, Massachusetts 02108-2892

BEACON PRESS BOOKS
are published under the auspices of
the Unitarian Universalist Association of Congregations.

03 02 01 00 99 98   8 7 6 5 4 3 2 1

Text design by Anne Chalmers
Composition by Wilsted & Taylor Publishing Services

Library of Congress Cataloging-in-Publication Data

Kriegel, Leonard, 1933–
    Flying solo : reimagining manhood, courage, and loss / Leonard
Kriegel.
        p. cm.
    ISBN 0-8070-7230-3 (cloth)
    1. Kriegel, Leonard, 1933—Health.   2. Poliomyelitis—Patients—
United States—Biography.   1. Title.
RC181.U5K75   1998
362.1'96835'0092—dc21
    [B]   97-28241

For My Brother,

ABE KRIEGEL,

And For My Cousin,

LEO BREITTHOLZ,

Who Held Me on Their

Shoulders Until I Could

Stand Alone

CONTENTS

FLYING
SOLO

"BEING DONE":

AN INTRODUCTION

"This courage stuff" sighs the boy from the cubicle across from mine, "it's a bitch." Like me, he is eleven years old, yet his sigh is that of an old man ready to acknowledge defeat. On this late afternoon of a warm day in early September, 1944, the resignation in that sigh is an accurate commentary on our prospects. More than half a century later, I cannot remember his name. But I remember the depths of defeat in that sound, as if I had heard it five minutes earlier, a wall of emptiness hovering in the air like a gray balloon leaking air. That boy was one of twenty-two of us quartered in a ward of the New York State Reconstruction Home in West Haverstraw. The ward was known simply as the Boys' Ward, and it was the place I would call home from mid-August, 1944 to early August, 1946. I think that the boy whose name I am unable to remember arrived at the Home three days after I did. I know that he was still there on the morning I left.

It was around four in the afternoon when he sounded his exasperation with "this courage stuff," a minor fact that seems important today, perhaps because in memory cause and effect are always important. We were each weary and beaten down. The two of us lay on adjacent stretchers, flat on our backs, exhausted by the most recent of our prescribed six-times-a-day immersions in the hot pool. The wheels of our stretchers were locked so that the stretchers formed a V pointing to the chrome slabs on which our bodies soon would lie once again. In a few minutes, we would each feel that hot water lapping our necks, shriveling world and body with the loss and pain being sweated out of us. As weary as those hot pool treatments made me feel, they were working. Six weeks after I lay in a small hospital in the Hudson River town of Cold Spring, my body as stiff as a newly varnished board, my legs were still lifeless—but the pain and stiffness were already being dissipated by the hot water.

Had I possessed a courage beyond my years, I would have reached over to grab that boy's hand in solidarity. I would have saluted his exhaustion and fear by acknowledging what we each understood—that our bodies no longer belonged to us, that we were in the process of "being done," flesh and bone and muscle cooked in the heated water, selfhood sweated out of us along with the pain and stiffness. But like all boys, my sense of solidarity with others was terribly limited. I was more afraid than imaginative back in 1944, more broken than brave. In those early days of learning to live with illness, everything I pushed up against challenged both my endurance and my pride. I was just beginning to realize that I was not as tough as I had thought I was before the virus struck. And so I didn't reach over to clasp his hand and I didn't say anything. I just leveled the ceiling with my eyes and thought about all that my body had been forced to surrender.

But I knew what it had cost him to acknowledge the need for courage, even if he had been speaking not to me but to the blind, ferocious malevolence of this universe whose terror neither of us could understand. His eyes had been on me when he sighed. Only now his eyes were looking past me, at the green tile border of the pool in which we soon were to be submerged again. Twenty minutes in the hot water, twenty minutes to recuperate from exhaustion on the stretcher.

That boy's eyes haunt me. I suspect they will haunt me forever. I remember not their color but how flat and empty they seemed, like glass washed to a smooth dullness by the ocean tides. We had to endure the heat one more time before therapy ended and we could be returned to the ward. Already depleted of energy and will, we readied ourselves for another session with the physical therapist, a blond graduate student from NYU who stood waist-high in the hot pool, nipples outlined against the wet gray bathing suit that encased her flesh like a surgical glove. Every time I would go back into the pool, I would find myself forcing my eyes from her breasts, objects of my prepubescent desire. She would touch me and poke me and urge me to concentrate on legs which had surrendered motion and were now surrendering pain—first through the hot packs wrapped around them during my first two weeks in the Home, then by these immersions in the hot pool. I was limber enough to sit up now.

In the polio epidemic that swept through New York in the summer of 1944, I lost the use of both of my legs. The boy lying next to me lost the use of his right arm and his right leg. Polio had "done us," a phrase that seemed as appropriate when I first heard it as it seems now. I first heard it lying in a bed in the rear of the ward, supposedly in isolation from the other boys in the ward, which did not prevent them from entering the room with impunity. Some were already long-term veterans of life in the ward, having spent a year or more in the Home. They arrived in the back room with the authority of boys pretending to a toughness they could not feel, sneering Cagneys and Bogarts in wheelchairs or walkers, fear stripping life down to a verbal swagger. How else could they acknowledge the reality of "being done"? The Boys' Ward boasted its casualty list—polio, arthritis, and osteomylitis crips, all of us "being done."

Passive in exhaustion, the damp smell threatening to smother me, I turn my eyes to the NYU therapist. At eleven, I am not sure of how men and women "do it." I only know that I want to do it, too. And that I am afraid. Leg muscles no more than an occasional twitch, I think of the therapist in the water working on me, as she is now working on a quiet city boy with a hangdog look and an olive-skinned girl from upstate who has a lovely smile. A year later, and I will lock wheelchairs with the olive-skinned girl behind the red-brick laundry, fumbling away at her as I try to forget dead legs in the soft feel of flesh beneath her gray wool sweater.

Like all healthy adults who live among sick children, the therapist is one of "them." Along with doctors and nurses, and the stretcher-bearers who live down the road in Garnerville, she seems to be from a different planet. For she possesses power over our crippled futures. She embodies the authority of hope. I believe she can breathe life back into my useless legs. Only now she is baking the pain and stiffness out of other bodies. I close my eyes, in no hurry to be submerged again in the hot water. My turn will come. Yet I cannot afford to recognize what really disturbs me. Will I ever be a man among men?

For a month, I am taken to the hot pool. At nine-thirty every morning but Sunday, the sessions begin. At noon, a stretcher-bearer brings me back to the ward for lunch. I return for my afternoon immersions at one-thirty. Each day sees me boiled and reboiled. Disease creates fixed routines, the first lesson a cripple learns. Illness is nothing but what it is—fact, condition, a message transmitted in pain and fear. Yet illness is not as singular as writers or cripples think. It provides the images that will shape my life, the reality out of which my future emerges. But illness is not dramatic. It is cloying, methodical, exhausting.

I am not Christian, yet I already think of my daily immersions as a baptism into the world of the crippled. An eleven-year-old boy weary with the necessity of going back into the hot water, I understand that to go back in that water is the best chance I have of ridding myself of the humiliation of illness. That boy and I will learn about the prospects facing us in the shadowy world of the crippled as well as the techniques with which to confront those prospects.

Why is the memory of that early September afternoon so embarrassing today? After all, I am not only a survivor but a man who can be said to have prospered. Yet remembering myself on that stretcher next to the hot pool makes me feel as if I were about to confess some dirty little secret in public. In a nation so in love with confession that it is as much at home with Oprah's diets as with Karen Finley's chocolate-coated flesh, atrophied legs are not sensational enough to command attention. Atrophied legs are not erotic. They cannot stand up to a crucifix that has been pissed on or the tattoos decorating Dennis Rodman's leaps of muscle and flesh. Yet there remains something in memory which touches on the forbidden. Who today believes that men should behave as men were expected to behave in 1944?

Be a man! An old, battered idea that has not fared well. Like all clichés, it embarrasses. Yet clichés spring from the cultures that give them life, and to the idea of what it meant to be a man in 1944 I owe my survival. If others can ignore such debts, I have no choice but to praise a salvation that is unfashionable if not subversive. What used to be spoken of as "manly behavior" is now considered laughable. It is difficult merely to speak of what is expected of a man in a nation in which one gender's victimization by the other is so embedded in our rhetoric that the word *manhood* has taken on a connotation that is reminiscent of certain four-letter words of my adolescence. But in 1944, six weeks into polio, I had lost the identity I possessed before the virus severed legs from will. If I could not admit that life as a cripple demanded courage in response, I was doomed. Yet the boy lying next to me had been right. This courage stuff was a bitch.

I still wonder what happened to him. He was the first boy I heard frame the need for courage as he acknowledged the fear that he wasn't up to the demands of illness. That he knew he had been "done" was evident in that sigh, a sound that spoke for every boy in our ward. At this point in my life, I no longer recall the faces of the boys in the ward: What I remember are the physical conditions with which they sallied forth into the world. Here dead arms tied in a sling basket, there legs as dead as my own. I still see wheelchairs racing through empty corridors, but as I stare into memory, a blankness of facial feature greets me, an absence of flesh and bone. Wheelchairs and prostheses remain the permanent consequences of illness.

That boy was trying to seize his twenty minutes of respite and suck up whatever resistance to his fate remained in his heart. Fear dominated his future, as it dominated mine. And his greatest fear was the fear of not measuring up to the demands of illness, of not being "man enough" to match the power of disease. Lying on a stretcher, waiting for his turn to go back into the hot pool, was terrifying to him, as it was to me. I was afraid of going back into that pool, afraid of just lying on the stretcher, afraid of the taste of the salt tablets I would be made to swallow as soon as I came out of the warm baptismal waters, afraid I would have to beg a God who filled me with rage ("Please, God, don't make me throw up!"). I was afraid not to beg. Most of all, I was afraid that others would witness my fear.

A man's body may be his castle, but it is first of all his body. I still shudder at what swallowing those wafers of salt—the memory of their taste fills me with nausea to this day—did to my sense of bodily worth. More than spinal taps or the urinals and bedpans from which the smell never quite washed away, the taste of those salt tablets embodies every humiliation of disease. To be an eater of salt was to be in the power of some dybbuk that had entered one's life unbidden. I endured the eating of salt as I endured the emptiness of night in the ward, my terror transformed into a desperate will to resist, as if at the core of the self was a reality illness could not change. It never occurred to me that I had any other choice but to protect that core. My hope was to take whatever fate would mete out—and to take it as a man.

In that hot pool, I would swallow pain, blink away discomfort, and eat salt until my useless legs were free of pain. That was what "being done" meant. In a dead time, I see two boys lying next to each other on stretchers, framing loss in memory. Silently, they pray to the blind malevolence, each afraid that the other will hear his prayer. They ask for the courage to get through the next immersion. They ask to be strong, to take not only this baptism but all the other baptisms awaiting them in the future. They ask to be "manly."

A nonbeliever's prayer, it was yet worth the price of learning. And it was answered, in a way. This book is about how it was answered—for it speaks of how one can endure the rage of loss, how memory creates debts out of loss, and how illness haunts memory forever. From the pain and humiliation illness insisted upon, I would define the man I was to be. I don't want to sound pompous or grandiose, only I don't know how else to phrase it. I do not believe that character is formed by illness. Life is process, and character forms and reforms, a truth as pressing upon writers as it is upon generals and physicians. I offer these chapters in the life of a man who asks for the reader's attention not because it is his life but because it is the only life he knows how to question. I am still trying to balance out the life I lived with the life

I was forced to leave unlived. There is memory and there is what memory leads to, the times and places and people that continue to speak to what I have had to pay in order to call my life my own.

One moves from memory to myth to places to people, and through it all one is still defining a self. And that is what we all must do, until the day we die. That I still affirm so traditional an idea of manhood surprises me. Yet that, too, is nothing more than a reflection of my own life. I believe it is a less anachronistic idea than we think. But let me leave it there. I had no choice but to take salvation where it was offered, and I feel no closer to the idea of manhood presented in John Wayne's movies than I do to the Jungian nonsense espoused by Robert Bly. Illness can cripple one's body, but it has a way of clarifying the mind.

I am still in the clutch of a memory. I still see those two boys lying alongside each other, citizens of an America in which no one spoke of "role models" and in which no one needed to create a reality that was "virtual." In 1944, fantasy and reality were distinct. Two cripples on the cusp of adolescence were being forced to acknowledge a future neither of them had envisioned. Yet if they knew that the future would be difficult, that they would need all the courage they could muster to confront it, they were lucky to live during a time when American boys, crippled or whole, expected eventually to become American men. There was still a war on, and if the price of survival was not the eternal vigilance of classroom posters warning "Loose Lips Sink Ships!" it was the belief that one could prove himself deserving of survival.

That boy next to me spoke of courage as a "bitch" because he had arrived in the Home already aware of what he might be called upon to pay. He knew, as I did, that the dead limbs of the other boys in our ward meant that their rage was as boundless as his. He knew, as I did, that we needed luck as much as we needed courage. And that we would have to learn how to organize pain into memory, how to give memory voice, and how to speak truthfully of all those losses the heart would carry within itself because of what had happened to the body.

PART I

MEMORY
AND
MANHOOD

1

FLYING
SOLO

I AM SITTING in my wheelchair at breakfast in the coffee shop of a hotel in Angel Fire, New Mexico. Only four other people are in the coffee shop, scattered throughout the large room. Like me, they are eating their breakfasts. But behind a glass partition that is up a flight of five carpeted steps is an adjoining room, half the length of a football field, where swarms of men and women attack tables piled high with pastries, muffins, pitchers of orange juice, eggs, fruit, and huge vats of coffee. These ravenous hungers all arrived at the hotel last night, having driven the one hundred and fifty miles north from Albuquerque. Their ballroom breakfast heralds the opening of the annual convention, scheduled to last three days, of an organization whose initials, APS, have been stamped in oversized gold letters everywhere one looks.

Some half dozen of the men, along with a dark-haired woman whose round pleasant face is lit by a wonderfully open smile, stand in a cluster before one of the tables. Dressed in tee shirts and white shorts covered by formal black jackets with tails, they seem as self-conscious as movie extras waiting for a casting call on the studio lot in early morning. They giggle and nudge one another, eye each other's black top hats with black silk bands and the invariable APS flashing in gold sequins even from their tee shirts. Before I arrived in the coffee shop, after I had returned to the hotel lobby following my two-mile run in the crisp early morning mountain air of Angel Fire, I had asked the young clerk at the front desk what the initials APS stood for. As if I were a college freshman pledging fraternity rush and he a fraternity brother assigned to serve as my mentor, he informed me that the hotel was hosting the annual convention of the Association of Principals and Supervisors of the Albuquerque public schools for the next three days. Aware of the significance of APS now, I wheeled into the coffee shop, past door after door covered by neat hand-lettered signs announcing meetings at which problems of curriculum development and drugs and pregnant teenagers were to be discussed later that day.

A very fat tow-headed morose-looking boy of eleven or twelve stands against the glass partition, next to a lean tall white-haired man, whose smile is fixed, confident. The smiling man, I assume, is the boy's father. The boy is wearing a psychedelic tee shirt, an explosion of color that bears the message, W H E N T H E D E V I L R E M I N D S Y O U O F Y O U R P A S T , T E L L H I M A B O U T H I S F U T U R E . The boy is bored and uncomfortable and out of place. He tugs at the man's sleeve. Smiling despite the boy's tugging, the man ignores him. The boy finally lets go of the man's sleeve and stands alone, staring through the glass partition, eyes searching out an emptiness beyond me.

I am drinking my second cup of coffee and studying a map of northern New Mexico, trying to figure out how my wife and I can drive to Cimarron from Angel Fire. There is a road, but according to my AAA map, it is a largely unpaved back road. My wife and I plan to lunch at Cimarron's splendid old Hotel St. James, where bullet holes from the guns of many of the Old West's most notorious gunmen are still embedded in the pressed tin ceiling. I look up from my map, to discover a woman dressed in blue dungaree shorts and white tee shirt, curiously unlettered. The woman has planted herself like a roadblock alongside my table. She stares at me without speaking for as long as thirty seconds. She is not embarrassed. She just stares, silently. Finally, she smiles, then says, "Do you mind if I ask you something?" Without waiting for an answer, she continues, "Do you mind if I ask you how you get around in that wheelchair?"

"I get around well, thank you," I say stiffly. Her sudden appearance has jarred my focus away from the map. I feel irritated, vulnerable.

"I watched you from my window this morning. When you were wheeling around the parking lot." I nod, irritation evaporating in the touch of vanity I feel at the thought of being observed as I do my morning laps. Because the hotel is built against the mountainside, the only place I am able to do my wheelchair run is in the parking lot. "My name's Dorothy," she continues. "Dot to my friends. I'm here with my husband for the convention. That's my husband, over there."

She points to a gathering of six or seven men huddling together near a microphone on a lectern. I am not certain which of the men she is pointing to as her husband, but I nod again. "He's a high school assistant principal. It's their convention. I'm just a teacher." She touches the chair directly across from where I am sitting in my wheelchair. "May I sit down?" she asks.

"Of course," I answer. She is slender, of average height, between thirty-five and forty is my guess. Her oversized tinted eyeglasses are the only note that she desires to be in fashion. When she sits down, I ask her whether she would like a cup of coffee.

"No thanks. I don't drink coffee." She stares at her fingers, looks up at the ceiling. Then she looks at me. "I asked about the wheelchair because of my brother," she explains. When I do not respond, Dot assumes that silence is an expression of interest. Or at least permission for her to continue. "He was in a wheelchair for five years."

"Is he still in a chair?" I ask. Now, I am interested.

"He's dead," she says. She frowns. "He died in 1978. In Albuquerque. On the Interstate, near the Tijeras Canyon cutoff. His car went off the road and plunged down the embankment."

"I'm sorry," I say. I know the interstate she is talking about, Interstate 40. And I know Tijeras Canyon. I had spent the summer of 1977 in Albuquerque, the summer I first fell in love with the mountains and high plateaus of northern New Mexico. In May of that year, I drove west from New York to teach a graduate seminar at the university. And for the next three months, I found myself exploring different patches of central and northern New Mexico. Day after day would see me drive off into small Chicano towns or else into those dark, lyrical mountains. I grew to love the vast New Mexican sky with its penciled sheets of rain that would evaporate before hitting the ground, just as, thirteen years earlier, while living with my wife and two-year-old son in the small Dutch coastal village of Noordwijk-Aan-Zee, I fell in love with the long gray horizon of the North Sea in winter. I used to drive the back roads of mountain New Mexico that summer, more often than not alone, reciting aloud those magic names whose sound would fill me with immense expectation— Chililli, Tesuque, Chimayo, Questa.

They had been doing a good deal of roadwork that summer, patching and widening I-40 as it cut through Albuquerque to feed itself to both east and west. The highway was chopped and rutted, divided into detours and speed zones. My dislike of the interstate system, a dislike that sprouted the moment I first emerged from the Holland Tunnel and turned onto the Jersey Turnpike, was magnified that summer by my search for ways to avoid the deadening prospect of driving for long stretches of time on I-40. For there had been a night when I, too, came perilously close to plunging into the canyon below.

I was driving east at dusk, to pick up New Mexico 14 North, a back road leading to Sante Fe. I was going to meet friends from the university for dinner at a restaurant a mile or so past the cut-off for Saandia Mountain. Suddenly, I was blinded by the lights of oncoming cars. Wheels spitting the loose roadside gravel, I fought panic as I forced myself to let the steering wheel play the spin out and saw my car skirt a road edge without barriers that bottomed into a precipitous drop. Like all narrow escapes, it proved an interesting topic to talk about later that night at dinner.

In the coffee shop, I want to hear more about how Dot's brother met his death plunging off the highway into Tijeras Canyon. But it is too awkward a subject to ask about. As if sensing my struggle, Dot smiles and leans forward. "It was night. It wasn't raining. But it was cloudy and dark. Very dark. No, he wasn't drunk. He wasn't on drugs either. Not that night, anyway. He came out of the curve and he simply drove right off the road and crashed. It was two hundred feet down." She pauses, looks over her shoulder at the group in which her husband stands. "They said it might have been suicide."

"Do you think it was suicide?" I ask. She is so forthright that I am now convinced that I can ask her anything without guilt or embarrassment.

"I don't *think* it was," she responds. "But I guess we'll never know for certain. Not in this life."

I had lived since the age of eleven, as those who are crippled must live, with the all-too-frequent burden of envy in my heart and a rage so encrusted on my soul that there were moments when I felt myself being physically picked up, as if by the hands of some invisible creature, and then held aloft, only to be squeezed into a consciousness created for me alone, the way I imagine the lovers in Rodin's *The Hand of God* felt thrust marble-cold into the blank unknown of the universe. And yet, I cannot remember a time when I thought, truly thought, about ending my life. I am intrigued by Dot's brother, intrigued by his fate, intrigued by the choice he may (or may not, my mind cautions) have made. I lean forward, as if I need to hear her more clearly. "How did he wind up in a wheelchair?" I ask.

"He was wounded in Vietnam. In 1973. He was twenty years old and he'd shipped over six weeks earlier. One night, his company got caught in a fire fight and he was hit. Shrapnel. Cut the nerves in his spine. They took thirteen pieces of metal out of his body. But there's nothing they can do about damaged nerves. He never walked again."

"I'm sorry," I offer, weakly.

She pauses, eyes blinking rapidly behind the tinted glasses. For a second, I wonder whether she is going to cry. Only she doesn't cry. "And you?" she asks. "What happened to you?"

"Polio," I say, embarrassed at how pedestrian the name of the disease must sound to a woman whose brother's body had been shot up in Vietnam. "When I was eleven."

She nods. "I guess I noticed you this morning in the parking lot because my brother was a big man," she says, "like you. And he used to work out, too. Watching you doing laps reminded me. He moved so quickly in his wheelchair. He drove a car. He always drove too fast. Even before he was wounded. As if he didn't want to miss out on anything, wheelchair or no wheelchair. He was learning to fly, too. Taking lessons. That scared us—me and my mother. We tried to get him to give it up. But he'd already flown his first solo flight."

As if I have been suddenly punched in the stomach, when I hear her say that her brother was learning to fly I take a deep breath, like a man about to plunge under water, desperate to fill his lungs. He had learned to fly. An extravagance of memory hurls me back to a time when I was not yet seventeen and I set out to create a self both I and the world could hold accountable. I remember drawing up a list of all the things I intended to accomplish over the coming years—a cripple's wish list for an impending manhood that is as powerfully rooted to memory today as most of its demands proved easy enough to meet in real life. Yet as distressing as that wish list now seems, remembering it reminds me that I was an American claimant. God knows, I took that list seriously. Like the young Jay Gatz, I made a list to remake a self, a blueprint for my total transformation. I wanted not to cease being the cripple I was finally able to acknowledge, but to pull selfhood out of the experience of being crippled, to rip it from a virus I already had personified as a living, malevolent being.

And the only item on that list I never mastered was learning to fly. That is why remembering it is so distressing. I tried. In my twenties, I went so far as to investigate the possibility. On a sunny afternoon in May, I drove out to a small airfield in northern New Jersey that a colleague had told me of to inquire about the possibility of taking flying lessons from the operator of a flight school. Only back in 1961, small planes could not yet be outfitted with hand controls, as cars already had been for decades. You needed your legs to maneuver a plane, the instructor said. Without the use of legs, learning to fly was impossible. Even for dreamers, reality remains the master.

In the years that followed, the responsibilities of adulthood multiplied and the normal life I had struggled for was marked off by a very traditional emotional topography. Love, marriage, fatherhood, the necessity of earning a living, travel, choosing schools for children, pursuing a career—these were proper boundaries for a man. Soon, I dismissed the idea of learning to fly as the kind of romantic adolescent desire that turned grown men in America into perpetual boys. Like most other normal American men, I would be content to leave the flying to others.

Only in this hotel coffee shop, I am seized by an overwhelming sense of loss. In my dream of flying, I could touch the healing emptiness of space. Now I suddenly feel growing anger at myself for never having learned to fly. And I am filled with admiration for Dot's dead brother, as if, in imagination's eye, I handed over to him the unfinished task I had once set myself. Before he plunged to his death over the rim of existence kissing I-40 and Tijeras Canyon, Dot's brother had learned to fly. And he had flown solo. The idea takes my breath away. It is a moment in which my fantasies of climbing mountains or hitting a baseball again or boxing again—of feeling the same absolute joy and confidence in my own physical being that I felt as a child, before polio struck—have not only come true but have come true, paradoxically, as I envision myself in the body of a fellow cripple. The Doppelganger had seized control, wrested ambition from memory, and turned his dead self into my fantasy made real. I should have wept tears of gratitude for her dead brother—so generous and beyond ordinary giving was he in the fulfillment he had allowed me to glimpse, if only momentarily.

For an hour, I listen to this woman who is no longer a stranger talk about her dead brother. I never do learn her full name (I don't remember whether she even offered it) and she never refers to her brother by name either. Throughout our conversation, her brother is "he"—name enough, as far as I am concerned. I want his presence to be as specific as the sense of debt taking root in my mind, but *he* has already assumed an existence beyond that of any ordinary mortal.

Dot herself has been born again, she informs me. Her conversion, I sense, springs from the time of her brother's death. She tells me of her faith in the Lord, her tone of voice curiously flat and mechanical. Indeed, she speaks much more passionately of her mission as a teacher of what she calls "communication arts" in an Albuquerque middle school than she does of her beliefs. When she asks me where I am going once I leave Angel Fire, I tell her that my wife and I plan to drive to Colorado Springs and spend a few days there before flying back to New York. She frowns, then tells me her sister and brother-in-law live in Colorado Springs. Only she is never at ease when she visits them. She does not like the Garden of the Gods. Seeing how puzzled I am when she says this, she adds, "As a Christian, there can be only one God. Our Lord and Savior."

But it is her brother, not her Lord and Savior, who has brought us together this morning. Dot is as willing to talk about him as I am eager to hear more about him. She tells me of how unusually cheerful her brother seemed when he came home from Vietnam. During the first months following his return, he would go off in his car or in a van he had purchased a share in with three other New Mexico paraplegics wounded in Vietnam, hurling himself into life with joy and gusto. "He was grateful to be alive. He would go trout fishing in that wheelchair. With other para vets. And how those boys laughed. I guess that's why it's so difficult for me to believe he drove over the edge deliberately."

She is still not certain of when the change in her brother took place. "He'd done drugs in Nam," she sighs. "But they all did that, didn't they?" She does not wait for me to confirm or deny that they all did it. Nor does it matter. Speculation about motive grants her no respite. The truth is, she confesses, they had never been able to wean him from drugs. Not really. Oh, he stopped at times. In fact, he hadn't been doing drugs for weeks before the night his car hurtled off Interstate 40 to plunge into the silence and space of Tijeras Canyon. Besides, drugs never are the cause. Drugs are the result. "Maybe if he had been able to accept the Lord in his heart," she says, wistfully. "But there was always too much rebel in that boy. He went his own way. Alone or with company, he went his own way."

In my eyes, going his own way is her brother's greatest triumph. But I cannot say that to Dot. The flying lessons, the fast driving, his knowledge—I insist upon this—of what he had become and of the opportunities he had turned his back on, above all, the need I sense in him to live day-by-day with the painful memories of what will never again be available. These are what I want for him. And what I want for myself. Even the aimless drift into drugs is understandable: his actions confirm the brother who now exists in my mind's eye. For me, it is his defiance, his refusal to live within the boundaries framed for those of us who are crippled, that make him a man I admire. But how do I tell this to the sister who grieves? How do I tell her that I understand why moderation, like seeking the Lord, could never be what her brother's cripple's heart searched for?

The answer is simple. I don't tell her. I just nod and silently understand that I have no right to define for Dot her brother's needs or her pain. For each of us, crippled or whole, there remains a single question that must sooner or later be answered: How much can you take before the taking itself overwhelms the desire for consciousness? And I have no answer to that. If I know nothing else, I have lived long enough as a cripple to know that.

"Maybe the change took place when he drove down to Central America in 1977," she suggests. "He went with a friend, another para. It's funny. He was in Mexico and then Nicaragua. You know, they're not supposed to like Americans in those countries. But they liked my brother. And he liked how they treated him."

"How did they treat him?"

"As if the wheelchair made him one of them. He said they made him feel as if life wasn't just about what he had lost. That's why he came back to Albuquerque."

"I'm not sure I understand," I say. Only I understand all too well.

"He didn't want to get too used to new possibilities. That's what he said. Does that make sense to you?"

It made a great deal of sense. But I didn't tell her that. I just shrugged, thinking of Dot's brother returning from Central America, probably with far greater bitterness than he had felt when he came back from Vietnam. Men grieve not for what they are but for what they have lost. Like his ambitions, a man's rage and pain are personal. It is not politics or religion or country that define a man but need—hard, insatiable, grasping, trying to push beyond the broken body, a slender reed stirring memory and desire, bending yet unbreakable.

"And then he drove off the road. Lost control of the car and just went off." She pauses. "I don't think it was suicide. But I'll never be sure. Sometimes, I think maybe he just grew tired of living. He was only twenty-five, but he wasn't the same after he came back from Nicaragua."

She gets up from the chair and stands in front of me, smiling. She leans across the table and offers me her hand. "I sense you're not a believer," she says. "But I want to leave you with the Lord's blessing."

"I'm not a believer," I admit, as I accept her hand. "But I'll take that blessing. Gratefully."

/ / /

That night, my wife and I meet two good friends from New York for dinner at the Angel Fire Country Club. "It's the best restaurant in Angel Fire," Harry says. "That may not sound like great praise. But it really is good."

Like me, my friend Harry had discovered New Mexico in the 1970s. The landscape somehow reminds him of the Austrian mountains of his pre-Hitler childhood. Two years ago, Harry and his wife Rosalind had purchased ten acres of still-wild mountain countryside between Angel Fire and Eagle Nest. Pleasure tinges the slight Viennese accent of Harry's speech as he describes the dirt road and the woods thick with aspen and underfoot the wild mushrooms that he and Rosalind pick and cook. We four, he insists, will eat dinner the next night in the apartment he and Rosalind are renting in a ski lodge near the hotel in which my wife and I are staying. "In the morning, Rosalind and I can pick mushrooms from the property. We'll have mushrooms and wine for dinner."

Harry and I have been friends for twenty-eight years. Like Dot's brother's death, our friendship is an outgrowth of the Vietnam War. It began with the first stirrings of the university antiwar movement in 1963, when we were both young instructors. It has continued ever since. Over the years, it has evolved into one of those friendships that seem as comfortable and in place as a family photograph on the living room wall, breeding manners and obligations from the history of what has been shared. Not merely time but events, large and small, the kind of history that makes the past personal. Anger over the war in Vietnam originally brought us together. Now we look at the world somewhat differently. That is politics. Real friendship has little to do with politics.

At dinner, I tell Harry and Rosalind and my wife the story of Dot's brother's death. As I speak, I watch Harry. Eyes attentive, his right hand strokes his goatee. More than anyone else I know, my friend Harry has remained intent on resisting the attractions of illusion. The clarity he asks for as a physicist is the clarity he wants as a man. Nothing is allowed to stand beyond explanation. Harry lacks patience with mysticism, insists that causality be clear and simple. Rational connections must be made. There are always rational connections.

Harry will not admit it, but there is a certain vanity to his pursuit of the rational—a price he pays in being unwilling to bend before mystery. Harry listens carefully as I try to piece together for him the story of Dot's brother's life and death. Harriet and Rosalind also listen. Only the story, as I tell it now, seems fragmented and almost senseless. I find it difficult to speak of how involved I felt in the life and death of that dead soldier whose name I do not know.

"Have you ever visited that Vietnam Memorial?" I suddenly blurt out. "Not the one in Washington. The one down the road here, between Angel Fire and Eagle Nest."

"I've been there," Harry says. "It's very moving. Very peaceful."

"It's funny," I say. "A few years back, I visited the Vietnam Wall in Washington. You walk along and you read the names of the dead. You read names at random. It was like acknowledging an entire generation. Far more moving than I thought it would be. But this chapel here. . . ." I pause, struggling for the right words. "It's so simple that it destroys history. The war was obscene. I've certainly never regretted opposing it. But when I visit the DAV Memorial, I want to believe it was a just war."

"It wasn't a just war," Harry says, frowning.

I nod. "But that doesn't stop me from wanting to believe it was."

/   /   /

In the valley below, space is like the long roll of ocean at sea—so that even clustered together the cattle seem scattered, oblivious to any other presence as only such dull-witted creatures can be, rooting themselves to the green grass of the lush hillside as if they have been frozen permanently into some Paulus Potter canvas. Standing on my crutches, my braked wheelchair to the left, I wedge my body against the rising concrete that soars grandly into the peaks of the two gull-like walls of the Disabled American Veterans Vietnam National Memorial.

Behind me, the dark mountains known as the Sangre de Christo evoke a sense of expectancy and threat, as they invariably do when I am in New Mexico. Against the horizon to the northeast, a lighter mountain range shields those small towns with names I have loved since the days of my childhood Saturday afternoon movie-going in the Bronx—Eagle Nest, Cimarron, Raton. An American landscape, as open in the space it claims as it is closed to the time it speaks of. Chicken hawks and a solitary eagle magnify the immensity of sky and valley and mountain that makes this landscape so extraordinarily beautiful as well as so intimately painful.

I am not, as Dot accurately sensed, a believer—not, certainly, in the Christ she knows as "Lord" whose blood is immortalized in the dark brooding mountains behind me. But each time I come back to New Mexico, I feel as if I am being filled with the harsh density of the universe, that unwavering flood of time and space before which I can only stand in awe and trepidation and which I still fearfully call on with names I claim I no longer believe in, names made familiar in childhood's ritualized fears and aspirations—Lord, King of the Universe, Melech, Adonai, Master, Creator, God of Mercy. Memory is not belief. I know that. Nonetheless, I remember.

There is an emptiness to New Mexico, even to a landscape as

lush and rolling and tranquil as this Moreno Valley spread out before me—and it is that emptiness which now fills me with fear. I am, after all, a product of New York's bustling streets. And much as I have come to love New Mexico since I first came here in 1977, I still dread its terrible capacity to inflict isolation. It is as if the price demanded for possessing all this space is that a man transform himself into insignificance, that he make of his own fear and loneliness a personal myth even as he makes of his defiance a religion. An emptiness of sheer dread that explains the wooden crosses of the Penitente flagellants I would spot thrusting out from the bare mountain ridges as I drove through northern New Mexico that summer of 1977—an emptiness in which the horror of flagellation was a dramatic posturing intended to affirm all that was human in the self because what was human had been momentarily dredged out of the greater horror of space.

Having moved in my wheelchair through the curving walls of the memorial chapel inside, I stand now in the bright New Mexican sun and watch it illuminate the valley below. Five o'clock on an early August afternoon. I feel admiration for the father of the dead lieutenant, that man who dedicated himself to building this monument to his son and to the twelve other Marines in his son's platoon, all killed in action in a single skirmish on May 22, 1968. Only a man overwhelmed by the demands of memory could have pursued so terribly painful a task. And pursued it so relentlessly. For it is not merely his dead son or the other dead Marines or the more than fifty thousand other Americans who died in Vietnam that this memorial honors. Nor is it those nameless hundreds of thousands if not millions of men and women and children in Vietnam who also died. It is memory itself, auctioneer of our obligations to what is human in the lives we set out to live, soothing presence before which we learn to prostrate ourselves not out of fear alone but out of need and recognition.

And as I gaze across this tranquil sun-drenched valley, I think of Dot's brother. I think of him driving swiftly through back roads leading from space into space. I think of him sitting in his chair in a mountain stream casting for trout. I think of him in Mexico and Nicaragua, at home even with his rage because he has learned what it is to be an alien in lands where even the natives are alien. I think of him coming back to Albuquerque and then losing himself, perhaps in the light of oncoming cars, perhaps in his own weariness, or perhaps—and this is what I would prefer in my own heart—in the satisfaction of having learned to fly and of knowing that once having flown solo into emptiness it will be easy enough to fly into emptiness again.

I do not know what took Dot's brother's car over the edge of the road to plunge into Tijeras Canyon. I do not want to know. Not really. Like Dot, I am willing to believe it was not suicide. In any case, that doesn't seem important. A man feels himself bend beneath the weight of what he owes others, as I now bend beneath the knowledge of the debt I owe that nameless wheelchair brother who learned to fly. My regrets for him are ordinary enough, the same regrets I would feel for anyone who died young.

I wish he could once again be stroked by the touch of a woman's fingers on his bare forearm. I wish he could once again smell the pinon smoke in the New Mexico he knew as a native and I have come to love as a stranger. I wish he could once again see the way the bursts of Indian Paint and Columbine still hug the edges of all those mountain roads he didn't drive off. I wish I could offer him everything in life that is physical and concrete and specific. I wish I could touch his life the way he has touched mine. For this was a man, a cripple like me, who had learned to fly. And in learning that, he had given me so much more than a gift of the senses.

Fearful of the pull of belief, I recite an unbeliever's silent Kaddish—praying to all the gods, for all the dead, in all the countries, in all our emptiness.

2

WHEELCHAIRS

''THE WHEELCHAIR was the way home.'' The line is taken from my first book, published in 1964, a time when I believed I was done with wheelchairs forever. I was thirty when *The Long Walk Home* was published, a husband and father, about to embark on a Fulbright year abroad. But the words younger men choose have a way of catching up to the realities older men must face. If the self-consciously dramatic tone I used to describe the origins of my love affair with the wheelchair is a trifle embarrassing today, the judgment itself remains surprisingly accurate. The wheelchair was, indeed, the way home.

For the first time I ever used a wheelchair was the moment I was given back the mobility I had surrendered six months earlier, when I lost the use of my legs. I was eleven years old, confined to bed, and about to discover why the wheelchair was to be the way home. In life, as in memory, that wheelchair proved as much salvation as I could claim during the twenty-four months I spent being remade as a cripple in the New York State Reconstruction Home.

/ / /

*I am once again an eleven-year-old boy sitting up in his bed
in the ward for boys between ten and thirteen. This ward has
been my home for five and a half months and I will live here
for another eighteen months. An explosion of joy sweeps
through my body as I look up and see my mother and father
and uncle. My father is pushing a wheelchair in front of him.
It is a few minutes after one o'clock on the last Sunday in
January 1945. Sunday is visitor's day. And as it does on every
Sunday, a sense of expectancy lingers in the air like the smell
of breakfast coffee. Every boy in the ward is breathing a bit
quicker, sensing the possibilities awaiting him on visitor's
day. On the edge of meeting a destiny that six months earlier
would have made me shudder, I feel prepared and grateful
and anxious. I am alive and I am to have a wheelchair of
my own.*

I had hungered for that particular possibility for two months,
ever since the hot pools to which I had been subjected from mid-
August until Thanksgiving succeeded in baking the stiffness out
of my body and left me with lifeless legs alone to worry about.
And my hunger was about to be fed. That wheelchair my smiling
father was pushing toward my cubicle was to open up the hospital and its grounds for me. Better still, it was to open up life as a
cripple for me.

It was a big, old-fashioned, straw-backed wooden wheelchair,
its oak arms gleaming in the frozen January sun that flagged the
ward and played the varnish shine as if it were some crazed
shadow dancer. My father, still a gentle immigrant after fifteen
years in this country, guided the chair alongside the bed in the
cubicle I had shared since September with a boy named Morty,
whose long narrow nose had earned him the nickname Mole-
man. Aided by my uncle, my father braced the chair against my

bed. "It's yours, Lennie," he said, voice filled with triumph. "We bought it for you."

No gift I would ever receive—not the baseball bat my uncle had given me for my birthday three years before polio struck, not the piece of yellow clay baked into the shape of an ashtray or candleholder I would receive twenty-three years later from my oldest son, crafted with a minimum of talent but with all the pride a four-year-old takes in being able to make what he gives—glows so brightly in my memory as that ponderous remnant of eighteenth-century rational design, that huge, ungainly, magnificently ugly throne on wheels.

We don't usually think of liberation as mechanical. The word strikes us as disreputable, tawdry, the very antithesis of liberation. *Mechanical.* One pushes the sound out of his mouth as it breaks off in midair, an impatient click that befits a forced, hurried exit. *Mechanical* leaves the mouth harshly. Link the word to any noun—*mechanical* freedom, *mechanical* style, *mechanical* abstraction, *mechanical* motion—and the implication is of something unearned, unimaginative, something for which one has not paid a proper price.

Yet it is accurate. That wheelchair was a mechanical gift that promised a mechanical liberation. And as I braced my hands on each side of its solid oak arms, and allowed my shoulders to take the weight of my body, slowly, cautiously, dropping into the seat, rear end meeting woven straw and wooden border, my back bracing itself against the slats of wood that made up the rear of the chair, I wanted to shout with joy for a happiness that was a jubilant, most unmechanical, gift. I wanted to bellow my liberation for the entire ward to hear. Ponderous and ugly and huge, this wheelchair was mine. And mine alone. Hands on its rims, I could feel possibility swell in the ward's steam-heated air. My father stood to the side, his joy matching mine, my uncle and mother smiling alongside him. Then my father nodded, as if offering a prearranged signal—and my hands moved as far back as my arms could reach and then thrust forward in unison as I rolled out of the cubicle into the ward aisle.

"It's my chair!" I shouted.

"It's Lennie's chair!" the other boys in the ward chorused, like a group of street urchins in a low-budget musical.

They were no more jealous than I had been two weeks earlier, when Morty had received a wheelchair from his parents. The war was still being fought in January 1945—like Archie Bunker, I still think of it as "*the* war, WW II, the Big One"—and most of the wheelchairs in the country had been sent, along with the green on the Lucky Strike cigarette pack, to help those who had been wounded in battle. Wheelchairs had been recruited for the duration. The only way you could get your own chair was if your parents managed to hunt one down and buy it. Wheelchairs, like meat, were rationed—subject to the demands of the nation's war effort. I suppose it is a simple irony that the war would prove highly beneficial for those of us destined to spend a lot of time in wheelchairs. Wars produce most of the truly significant advances in orthotics and prosthetics. Among its gifts, "the Big One" gave us the folding wheelchair, constructed out of steel and chromed to as striking an example of functional design as a racing car in the Indy 500. But chrome and vinyl and anodized aluminum were still in the future. In 1945, I was overjoyed to push that big, ungainly varnished wood and woven straw Packard of a wheelchair.

I loved that wheelchair with a passion that embarrasses me to this day. A man should love god or women or his children or the smell of salt air on the beach or his country or books or good wine or rare steaks. A man should love baseball and fishing and stamp collecting and Vermeer's *View of Delft*. But a wheelchair? A wheelchair should be nothing more than a necessary interlude in a man's life, a comic substitute for useless legs or arthritic bones. And yet, I truly did love that wheelchair, so wholly, so absolutely, that the memory of such a singular passion still takes my breath away and makes me giggle like a schoolboy.

What a gift of overwhelming freedom that chair endowed me with. After months of going from bed to therapeutic hot pool and back again pushed on a flat mattress-smelling stretcher by a hospital orderly, I was enthralled by my newly won mobility. Within the week, I had been transformed into a wheelchair addict, spinning joyously through the long gray corridors of the hospital, pushing myself over the small hills and pebble-encrusted grounds as if I were an explorer making his way across some unknown continent. Like a tank driver, I maneuvered my chair's bulky presence down the rutted dirt road that led from the hospital to Letchworth Village, a state home for the mentally retarded that we boys, our verbal cruelty as much a mark of our crippled state as our wheelchairs and braces and crutches, derisively called "Crazytown." I had my first experience of adolescent sexual passion in that wheelchair. And in that wheelchair, I played baseball and basketball and Ping-Pong, ignoring even the memories of the athlete I had been in the sheer joy of once again swinging a bat, even if I was seated in a chair. I first learned to shoot craps in that wheelchair, bending low outside a toilet stall in the ward lavatory (the first "wheelchair accessible" toilet stall I would know) as one of the other chair-bound boys blocked the entrance as guard, ready to yell "Chickie the nurse" as soon as the enemy was spotted, my left hand holding the left rim of my chair for balance even as my right hand rubbed the dice against the spokes of the wheels for luck. In that wheelchair, I dashed off to my daily physical therapy sessions, raced other boys to the schoolroom in which we were confined for an hour and a half each afternoon. My chair was a throne on wheels as it held me in solitary splendor in the dark hospital auditorium each Friday night, where I sat through the weekly movie that fed an already overly rich fantasy life.

The wheelchair was the way home. And in August 1946, the way home needed no more pointers. I had my wheelchair, which I had used for a year and a half. I had my long-legged braces tied around my middle by a leather pelvic band. I had my adjustable wooden crutches. In short, I was as reconstructed as the New York State Reconstruction Home could make me. One early August morning, an ambulance pulled up in front of the ward to take me home. The first thing that I remember doing after I arrived home was to get out of my chair and walk through that small apartment in the Bronx on my braces and crutches. I was thirteen years old, a soft fat boy who knew that he was unprepared both for the adolescent years ahead of him and the toughening-up process he would need to get through those years. Yet I also knew that the apartment was an older home than the ward I had lived in over the past two years—an older home that was yet a place of beginning again, where my wheelchair did not belong.

Even then, I understood how much I owed my wheelchair. Racehorses whose careers are finished are put out to pasture and old dogs spend their last years as beloved pets, however mangily odiforous, allowed the run of the house. These are the proper rewards of love and service. Had I possessed a stronger sense of style, I would have blessed and then burned that wheelchair in some sort of public ceremony, the way the Vikings burned their long ships as funeral pyres. I would have acknowledged the gifts of freedom and movement it gave me during the eighteen months I spent in it. And I would have totaled my debts to that chair through an emotional arithmetic that might truly match the value of all that it had presented me with. The mobility it offered had fed my need for exploration and adventure. My chair had framed the sense of possibility a crippled child needed so desperately. A wheelchair helped make me, as it helped make so many of the boys in that ward, adaptable—and adaptability would prove the most valuable trait a cripple could possess.

It is a night in May after dinner in the ward. In a few months, I will return home. But for now, mine is one of eleven wheelchairs making their way to the small town about a half mile down the road from the hospital—an invasion which will result in our being restricted to the ward for a week and which immediately is absorbed into our myths of defiance of the "normal" world. We are eleven boys in wheelchairs and we are matching ourselves against the collective authority of doctors, nurses, and townspeople—all those whom we have thought of as the "others" ever since our own arrival into the world of the crippled. In the soft twilight, we know we will be punished. But we are proud of ourselves, we are happy, we are not supplicants. At least, not for the moment. Huck Finn has his Mississippi and his raft. We boys have this half mile of poorly paved country road—and our wheelchairs.

The wheelchair was the way home.

But I didn't burn my wheelchair in some mock Viking funeral. For the next year, it stood jammed into the corner near the window of the room I shared with my younger brother. I swore off it, rather dramatically, I must confess, promising aloud to that God I already claimed to scorn that I would never again use it—not,

at least, as a wheelchair. Only I couldn't give it up. Not altogether. Perhaps it was an emblem of my need, a token of the defiance that linked me to that hospital ward where one did not
need to confront the "normals" because in our crippled society
they didn't matter. At least, we liked to pretend they didn't. And
so I still used it—but used it now as an armchair, seating myself,
like some young Buddha, against that slatted wooden back, my
eyes surveying the street below the window.

Two days after Christmas, even as my two years in the Home
receded in memory, all of New York, including the street below
my window, was buried beneath the most severe blizzard in the
city's history. That blizzard was to bring twenty-six inches of
snow to the streets of the Bronx. And the snow would pack and
ice over throughout a long, cold, gray winter. For the city, the
blizzard would be transformed into a legendary event. But it
would make me a shut-in until the end of March. And once
again, my chair would service my needs. I sat in that demobi-
lized throne, gazing out over the bleak, desolate, snow-crusted
street, banking the memory of that long-ago May invasion of a
small country town, because only memory could deny the frozen streets and make reality palatable.

But after every winter, spring must come. The ice broke, the
snow melted, and one late-March day the long winter was over.
And with the end of winter, my hibernation also ended. I learned
to get downstairs, at first boosting myself on my hands to move
from step to step on my rump, then teaching myself to walk up
and down the stairs on my crutches. Although I had been away
from the city for two years, I quickly readapted to its temptations. The street became an extended living room. I no longer
needed to sit by the window and observe life below. As the world
began to open up, the wheelchair that stood in such ponderous

isolation by the window turned into a visible anachronism, a reminder of that past I was determined to move beyond. That August, a year to the day of my return, I asked my father to get rid of the chair. He pushed it up Bainbridge Avenue and donated it to Montefiore Hospital five blocks away. I was a crutchwalker now.

And I swore, aloud, as solemnly as only adolescent boys can swear, that I would never again use a wheelchair. No oath I ever made seemed more serious. Nor more clearly earned. As I forced my body to adapt to the prospects before it, I came to feel a curiously self-righteous contempt for the eighteen months I had spent in that chair, as if acknowledging the pleasures I had experienced as a wheelchair rider had somehow cheapened the drama of battling illness.

Crippled or not, I was a pure product of this America, weaned on the pragmatic sense of possibility all Americans like to think of as theirs by right of birth. But in my case, at least, that much-vaunted pragmatism disguised my true passion, the need to surmount whatever was difficult, to prove my worth by overcoming all obstacles in my way. I was at my most American in my determined insistence that a man could satisfy ambition with individual acts of virtue—his own manly virtue. To test oneself was as American as a hot-dog eating contest on the Fourth of July.

I had taken an oath, renounced ease, promised myself that I would earn the endurance needed by a crutchwalker, no matter what the cost. If nothing else, the throbbing sensation in my shoulders after I forced myself to walk on braces and crutches through the streets of the Bronx for three or four miles confirmed the transformative power of pain. Pain was an indication of tenacity. "The tougher, the better." "No pain, no gain." "Show 'em what you're made of." Like every other cliche thrust before those who were crippled, such slogans told me that I was expected to content myself with aching muscles and throbbing shoulders. These were proof enough of my worth as a man—or so one crippled adolescent believed. I had to "earn" even the right to claim my disease through public acknowledgment of a private condition, just as I had to earn the right to call myself "cripple" through my performance as a man on crutches. I had to see myself, as well as be seen by others, as being in the American grain.

As I reconstructed my life, I refused to think about a wheelchair as an alternative to walking on braces and crutches. In fact, I avoided thinking about wheelchairs at all. On those few occasions that I spotted a chair coming toward me on the sidewalk, I felt threatened, as uncomfortable as a card shark at a public session of Gamblers Anonymous. I would fix my eyes on the horizon beyond the chair. If it were possible to do it without being too obvious, I would walk across the street to avoid confronting the temptation of being a wheelchair rider once again. Not that I refused to acknowledge a fellow cripple. My refusals were deeper, more complex. I could acknowledge man or woman. What I couldn't acknowledge was the wheelchair in which they might be sitting.

And all the time, I hyped my hunger for the "normal" by telling myself that abstinence from the ease a wheelchair promised me was "healthy" (all abstinence, to my fiercely puritanical adolescent mind, seemed healthy at that time), an imperative of any successful rehabilitation. I wanted what those who have undergone great change invariably want—to be both a singular presence and, at the same time, to be like everybody else. How eager I was to prove myself worthy of the admiration of the "normal" men and women I saw in my neighborhood. I soon learned to despise such conventional desires. But if you hunger after what others assume as a right, you make yourself over in the image of those others—no matter how poorly the suit fits or how twisted the tie knots. There is a peculiar violence to need, particularly when it lies beyond the scope of one's ability to define precisely what one's need is. First, I discovered that violence. Then I embraced it.

Yet I do not want to place too great a psychological burden on my need to be a crutchwalker. The truth is that walking on legs encased in steel and leather, crutches beneath my shoulders, really was preferable to sitting in a wheelchair. It wasn't so much that I myself believed this but that I, like almost every boy I lived with during my two-year hospital residency, had absorbed it into the psychic economy of a cripple. The belief that using a wheelchair signified some sort of spiritual surrender had been absorbed into all that I believed made a man a man. "No pain, no gain!" I am still stunned at the ease with which I was able to accept such banalities, even more stunned when I recall how often I hear them bruited about today—in gyms, sermons, televised football games. And yet, even more amazing is the knowledge that, in some quiet corner of my mind, I still believe in those banalities—passionately.

I would be lying were I to write that rejecting the wheelchair didn't prove valuable. By any standard, mine was a strikingly successful example of physical rehabilitation. In many ways, I remain a textbook case on how a man can adapt to physical adversity. Had I remained in a wheelchair, I suspect I would have settled for whatever easier options were available. But in some corner of my being where logic succumbs to fear, to continue using a wheelchair would have seemed a terrible surrender. My task was simple: I had to learn to be my own hero, my own role model—which is another way of saying that I had to learn to live with neither heroes nor role models.

Walking on braces and crutches endows a man with a peculiar vanity as well as with a remarkably vivid sense of the possibilities of bodily grace. It may prove a surprise to those who are not crippled, but a man can feel like a prince of his own making while walking on braces and crutches. He can go as far as the strength in his arms and the rage in his heart allow. The most intimate of embarrassments, it is, as Hemingway said of bravery and courage, probably better not spoken about. But the vanity of walking on braces and crutches offers a man a certain sense of his own durability. A wheelchair is different. It is difficult for any man to feel truly brave in a wheelchair, for it is difficult for him to acknowledge the profound, often painful, difference between those who sit and those who stand. A crutchwalker knows that he *needs* those braces strapped to his legs and those crutches beneath his shoulders—but they are *his* legs on which he is standing. And he *is* standing.

At thirteen, I got out of my wheelchair. A year later, I got rid of it. At thirty-three, I was forced back into a wheelchair for six weeks. A freakish accident (all accidents are freakish in memory) that I would laugh about as the years passed. But a warning, too, of what the future held. I would never laugh at that.

I am walking the baby-sitter home. It is a windy night in late October. The baby-sitter lives in the apartment building across the street. The wages of baby-sitters in New York in 1966 are fifty cents an hour and being escorted home. I drop her off at her apartment, say good-bye, and make my way back to my own building. It has begun to rain, hard, the wind scooping the street's hollows with gusts that drench me. I hurry on my swing-through gait across the street. As I hurtle through space to jump the curb the way I always do, a sudden gust of rain and wind slaps against me. Afraid of losing my balance, I stab the night air with my left crutch and it comes down not on the concrete sidewalk but on . . . a banana peel! Chaplinesque wind-me-up-and-throw-me-down doll spins through rain and darkness until my outstretched left arm breaks not the fall but my wrist. You cannot walk on crutches with a broken wrist.

The wheelchair was the way home.

I had been down that way before. And not just in the wheelchair. Polio had left me like a fighter perpetually in training for his comeback. The return match was what I dreamed of. It was both fate and identity. I had constructed a balance sheet of triumph and defeat from memories of the normal boy I had once been. As a consequence, I learned early on that the price that is demanded of the cripple for success is that he always be prepared to perform. "Show 'em what you're made of" was not merely a cliche; it was also a religious catechism for one's burgeoning ego.

Yet however much I might dream of my comeback, I learned that a cripple, even a successful cripple, is like a talented but punchless boxer. He soon learns that style alone is insufficient. Not even an intelligent and courageous fighter can get by on style alone, just as no cripple can get by solely on the determination to outdo the individual who is not crippled in the game of being "normal." One soon recognizes the difficulty of pretending one is keeping on even when one does not want to keep on. And as one grows older, it becomes increasingly difficult to ignore the fact that one's inner being has grown tired—tired of defiance, tired of resistance, tired of the daily grind of trying to take pleasure in what has become mere routine. The difficulties do not usually stem from the natural losses to which flesh and bone are heir. Forget what has been written about post-polio syndrome, forget the accidents that beset all of us as we age. Those are simply the spin of the coin. Mortality may be a disease, but it is a disease shared by all men and women. I am talking, rather, about losing one's inner self, one's drive. I am talking about the danger of losing one's sense of purpose. For when a man loses those, he loses courage. Only in literature does suffering ennoble. In life, it just wears one down, until one reaches the point where all that can be said is, "To hell with it!"

Admittedly, "To hell with it!" reverberates with as true a ring of cliché as "No pain, no gain!" or "Show 'em what you're made of!" Like all clichés, it tells a man more about why he is the way he is than he would like to admit. "To hell with it!" is an acknowledgment of a sense of outrage, the cry of an individual who has faced expectation too often and who has realized that when certain skills begin to erode, determination and effort and discipline will no longer do the job. They are simply no longer sufficient. One is all blown out, finished. The will is dead, exhausted, like the will of Roberto Duran when he failed to answer the bell after the eighth round of his title fight with Sugar Ray Leonard. Unable to defy fate any longer, he finally cried out, *"No más."*

I find it curious that Duran's *"No más"* immediately labeled him a talented fighter who lacked heart. For a man who carries the memory of a wheelchair as temptation's own seductive goddess, Duran's *"No más"* seems, rather, the remark of a fighter overwhelmed by the excessive demands he had made upon himself. One might more accurately speak of him as a fighter finally overwhelmed by the courage demanded of the self. Only an individual finally prepared to allow himself to give in to fate can say, "To hell with it!" Only someone ready to acknowledge that the body has finally reached the point that one has always been terrified it will reach—the point at which skill and training and determination and defiance have been exhausted and have become warring cancers battening off each other—can accept the urge to say, *"No más."* Think of what it takes to leave the mind emptied of all illusion. Think of how even the idea that one has resisted fate valiantly must finally be surrendered. Nothing is left except the weariness of once again trying to resist the temptation to give up. The ego is stripped even of the surrender lurking within. It was not heart Duran lacked—it was memory.

I used to wonder precisely what goes through the mind of a fighter down on the canvas, as he listens to the referee counting him out while he tries to work up enough strength of purpose, what we like to call courage, to get back on his feet. Now I think I know. It is not defeat a fighter fears as he hears that count; and it is certainly not the consequences of defeat. Those consequences may even seem welcome as he lies on the canvas, struggling within himself. It is that the ending he has always feared is on the verge of finally arriving. No more metaphors exist with which he can shield the self from its imminent demise. "To hell with it!" Why not? Over, done, finished. Revelation is at hand. If not for the audience, at least for one's own self.

It was not the mundane events of aging that brought me back into the wheelchair. The broken femur of my right hip, the carpal-tunnel syndrome in my left elbow, the fractured index finger that made gripping crutches difficult—these all would send me back into a wheelchair for short periods of time. And it wasn't simply that as I moved into my mid-fifties, I began to feel as if my sense of balance had cut loose from my crutchwalker's grace, as if it had been waiting for the opportunity to take off on its own and leave me to my own scheming. Aging is inevitable; and I never had any illusions about that.

But accident and aging only explain my intermittent returns to the chair. What they do not explain is how my mind began once again to embrace the image of the wheelchair rider I once had been. They do not explain how, as I would walk toward the faculty dining room of the college at which I taught, I would see, not ghostlike and stripped of dimension but solid and secure and tempting, an image of that huge straw-seated wooden-backed hulk that had set me free so many years ago. Was it merely a vision my inner man desired? Or one that my fate now demanded? I don't know. Neither truly explains my weariness at the prospect of living up to my own idea of who I was and what I could still do with my life. "To hell with it!" explains that. Were I a fighter who had thrown everything he had into the possibility of triumph and still come up short—tired, inadequate, beaten— then *"No más"* would explain it, too. The wheelchair was no longer a mechanical liberation—it was now a fitting metaphor for where I was and how I had managed to get there.

Getting back into the wheelchair was not the spiritual death I feared. It may be that a touch of shame accompanied it. I'm not sure, although I confess to the lingering suspicion that I made the move too early, that I might still have had a few years of walking on braces and crutches left—no matter how difficult the effort. No one knows better than I that the way a man views the world standing is different from the way he views it sitting in a wheelchair. Modesty, false or earned, has no place in my equation. Simply put, no one of my acquaintance, neither man nor woman, had a better right than I to tap his body on the shoulder and say, "Well done . . . but enough." And that being the case, let me add that I don't know anyone who has a better right to have come to that point in his life where it seems suitable to say, "To hell with it!" It is that simple, and that complex. For more than forty years, a crutchwalker, and now, a wheelchair rider again—in reality, as in memory.

3

A FEW
KIND WORDS
FOR ANGER

LIKE SO MANY writers of prose, I started out with the intention of becoming a poet. Unfortunately, ambition is rarely the mother of talent, and by the time I was a senior in college, I knew that while poetry might be my passion it was not going to be my mistress. Yet after confessing my lack of talent as a poet to myself, I was left with a number of bad poems in my possession, more than I thought it possible for anyone to have written. And each of those poems was a testimonial to a young man's need to bare soul and body in verse.

As confessions go, this is probably tepid stuff. Even literary confessions need a certain *sturm und drang* quality, a beating of cymbals and drums, in order to be interesting. Confessions should be drawn from bone-deep, scandalous memories. Still, I ask to be trusted in this: as bad as those youthful poems were, I could never surrender them to the waste-paper bin that is a writer's truest friend. Literate enough to know that my college poetry deserved to be burned or drowned or at least made the object of public ridicule, I saved my poems not because I harbored a secret conviction that the work was better than it was or because I believed in my heart that my poetry was a victim of the pedestrian taste of a meretricious time. I may not be a poet, but even writers of prose are smart enough to distinguish hawk from handsaw. I felt no twisted affinity for the failed ambitions of youth—not even when they were my own ambitions. But if one learns nothing else as a writer, one learns that it is possible to hold on to certain aspects of the past simply because they once seemed so incredibly intense.

Yet why do I still hold on to that juvenilia? Obviously, not because I believe it worthwhile poetry. Still, as I comb through that verbiage, I find a stray line or two that speaks to who I was and what I thought when both the world and ambition were younger. Occasionally, I even find myself re-rereading entire poems, only to be struck by how many of the lines I wrote at nineteen were written in praise of anger. Anger was my greatest passion back then. But even in my current confessional mode, I remain much too self-conscious to quote most of those lines. Permit me, then, to offer a single line strolling through memory like imagination's shop steward counting heads at a union local: "Anger is man's least primitive state." Admittedly, it's not much of a line. Pretentious, even sententious—yet it is representative of the kind of thing I was writing in the 1950s. I nod approvingly whenever I reread that line, for nothing better embodies my sense of how a man was supposed to approach the world during my years of adolescence and early manhood. At nineteen, I believed in the sentiment—I'm much too embarrassed to speak of it as an idea—behind that line. And I believed in it absolutely. At the risk of being dismissed as a perpetual adolescent, let me admit that I believe in it still, that I cherish, more than ever, the meliorative effects releasing anger has had on my life. Having tried to live with anger and having tried to purge myself of it, I find that living with it is not only more honest, but more respectful of the kind of life I claim for myself.

/ / /

Both anger and its offspring, rage, have received a poor press in America, no doubt because they are emotions which violate the reflective temperament that we still insist on as the ultimate aim of education and maturity. When it is visibly displayed, anger makes us uncomfortable, for it reveals the self on the verge of moving out of control. Most Americans prefer to deny the existence of that self, or at least prefer to ignore it. A nation of therapy junkies, Americans are more and more obedient to pop merchants who advise them on how to "overcome anger," who insist that emotions must be "channeled," who believe that rage and anger are tasteless leftovers from the nation's suppressed Puritan past. In our national psychobabble, the display of anger is considered valid only to the extent that one can "make emotion work for you." Anger is a kind of spiritual leak which demands a plumber to repair it as quickly as possible. Yet after the leak has been repaired, one is faced with the problem of how to get rid of the plumber. Otherwise, one is going to wind up paying him overtime. As for rage, the less said about it, the better. Rage is too dangerous even to think about.

Anger is acceptable when it leads to passivity. Otherwise, It is considered illegitimate, an emotion which can be handled only if one transforms it into what is good and wholesome and positive. Yet those poems indicated that there was another idea working on me in college. At nineteen, I looked upon anger as an emotion that might yet lift me up and help me survive the way I believed a man was supposed to survive. Messy and unkempt and uncontrollable, it was the only emotion that might help me get through an excruciating period in my life. Anger allowed me to survive not only a writer's confrontation with memory, but the painful recognition of how different my past was from the past I found myself dreaming about long after I thought I had made my peace with the leavings of disease.

When I was in college, there was a lyricism to the anger I felt that made the emotion seem even more intense. That lyricism remains most vivid in my recollections of the way I experienced anger, in the way it purged passivity and picked my soul up from out of its quiesence. It may be that the lyricism made the emotion more dangerous than it seemed at the time. It was certainly different from that emotion recollected in "tranquillity" Wordsworth urges poets to seek in their memories of childhood. Yet I soon discovered there was much to be said for an emotion that insists men behave the way men are supposed to behave, especially in an age as eager to embrace cultural relativism as ours. To speak of the boundaries of manhood, of how a man was expected to behave and think, can inspire ridicule today. Yet those boundaries not only exist, they are also distinctly and painfully personal—which is *why* they cannot simply be laughed out of existence.

Anger's origins are as specific as they are harsh. The loss of my legs to polio in 1944 occurred at the same time that the most devastating war in history was killing millions of men, women, and children in Europe and Asia. Yet try to censure memory with reminders of the millions dying on this battered planet, speak of all who suffered far worse than useless legs, talk of Auschwitz and Hiroshima—and you will receive no greater response than my irritable, "So what?" Does it matter that others have suffered more? My anger is *my* anger, my suffering *my* suffering. I brood about Bosnia as much as my neighbors do—but were I a Bosnian whose life had been ripped apart by ethnic and religious insanity, I would get down on all fours and howl at the moon like a crazed dog. What happens to a man or woman is important *because it happens to that individual.* The polio virus that took my legs took them from my body. (Among the virtues of anger is that it imposes identity on both friend and enemy while making the abstract personal, so that I came to speak of an invisible organism as *my* virus, just as I gave it face and body and malignity.) It shredded the balance of my life. And it thus became a fit recipient for my anger. Anger and rage are invariably personal—and what I felt for that invisible organism was felt because of what *it* had done to *me.*

It was anger that allowed me a different kind of negative capability from what the literary critics speak of. Simply put, my anger insisted that I refuse to resign myself to the triumph of my virus. To do that would have been to give it the victory it wanted. "Do not go gentle into that good night," urged Dylan Thomas, a better line, offering far better advice, than my own "anger is man's least primitive state." Yet with anger as teacher, I learned how much better it felt and how much healthier it was to "rage against the dying of the light" than to accept what fate or God or chance had meted out as my proper due.

For the good advice Thomas offered in his plea to a father facing death turned out to be even better advice for a son doomed to live—and, it turns out now, doomed to live for more than fifty years—with the aftereffects of illness. Anger kept me from surrendering to the arbitrary whims of the future by insisting that I not make myself part of my own defeat. Anger offered me the possibility of resisting the victory of my virus. It allowed me to refuse to permit that virus to transform the power it had gained over my body into power over my heart and mind. That it took its toll, that it has dominated the landscape of my mind, is beyond dispute. Yet that, too, was at least part of what I had been trying to say when I called it "man's least primitive state." And anger helped save a life in which rage proved as powerful therapy as any cripple could ask for, allowing me to confront the legacy of disease honestly.

/   /   /

On some level, I have been an intimate of anger ever since I realized that the loss of my legs was permanent, that I would never, as the whisper in my mind phrased it, "get better." There would be no appeal to a higher court. I simply could not face the prospect of living out the rest of my life unable to walk and run. And I managed to avoid thinking about that prospect until a month before my seventeenth birthday. The idea that what my virus had done to me was permanent and unalterable did not strike home until an April morning in 1950. Until then, I fantasized about my future but managed not to think of it. "Just do it!" was not yet one of America's slogans back then. My slogan was, "Just don't think it!" Today, that Saturday morning is fixed in memory as a point of beginning again. In a scene crystallized by the release of my pent-up rage, I still can feel the press of thwarted dreams in the drift of memory. I would soon master the art of viewing my own body as somebody else's property. But memory must stand as the way it was. Or would yet be.

The young man lies in bed. Bored, restless, confined to a damp mattress because of an outbreak of boils on his thighs which makes it too painful to strap on his braces and go downstairs to the sun-drenched street, the young man has been lying in bed for two days and is trying to figure out how to get through this sunny Saturday. First, he considers reading the book on the night table next to the bed, which his brother took out from the library on 204th Street. The book is a historical novel, Captain from Castille, *and the young man knows that he can drift into its promise as soon as he opens the first page. He has already read the book, and knowing what is to happen can vivify fantasy. Yet he has begun, of late, to feel shortchanged by all such seductions.*

The young man's bed is jammed against the living room window of the small apartment. He looks down at the street below, where a stickball game is in progress. A smell of creosote and gasoline and grass, mixing together, works its way through the open window and fills his nostrils. Despite the smell, despite his irritation, the morning air is as soft as a woman's hand across his cheek. He sees the stickball game in the street. He feels tense, sullen, a victim of his victimization. Among the players are both his closest friend and his younger brother. He yawns, shifts uncomfortably on his ass as a slash of pain reminds him of the two thick boils beneath his right hip, ready to burst.

And then, just as his thirteen-year-old brother strides to the manhole cover serving as home plate to slash the air with a practice swing, the truth hits him — a reality so clear that in the future it will freeze into an image more powerful than illusion. He is a cripple! And he will never play ball again because playing ball is not what cripples do. He has been marked out, defined by what he will never again be able to do. His mind as assaulted as his body, the young man hears a whimper in the air. He is stunned as he realizes that the whimper has come from his own mouth, rising like a cloud of sound from the sour depths of anger beyond consciousness. Oblivious to the searing pain of boils on hips and thighs, he sits up in bed, then begins to pound his fists on the windowsill, weeping with rage, trying to obliterate time in the crush of knuckles and hands on wood and stone.

It may be that the realization that what my virus had wrought was permanent had been lurking at the back of my mind for months or even years. I still can't say for certain. I had already lived with what the virus had done to my body for almost six full years, so I must have had some idea of what the life awaiting me would be like, no matter how strong my fantasies were. Why reality broke through on that warm spring morning is an open question, for memory can never go unchallenged where disease and its consequences are concerned.

What is not open to question is the explosion of rage that swept through my life that morning. Finally, the ability to admit to myself that I would never again feel the power of legs that were healthy had given anger permission to erupt like some long-dormant volcano. I did not know then that the eruption would lead to the first truly honest assessment of my situation I would make. For fifteen minutes that seem in memory closer to fifteen hours, I was literally crazed, so enraged that I slammed fists against windowsill until my knuckles were scraped raw and bloody. Why I didn't break my knuckles and turn the hands that would carry me into real life to jelly seems, at this point, miraculous. Or, at the very least, unexplainable. Were I a believer, I might accept that as explanation enough. But at the time, the idea that I would have any sort of future was the last thing on my mind. All I hoped to feel was this blessed rage. Pounding that windowsill, I sobbed, cursing my fate and God and life itself, until I fell back against the pillow, exhausted and empty, as if the boils had burst in concert.

An exhaustion so total that I felt as if I were being scrubbed down for my impending death, body and mind so wiped out that they seemed to drift before my inner eye like bubbles of another existence. To feel simultaneously both rage and detachment from one's inner self was curiously exhilarating. I was dizzy with the rush of liberation, as if those bleeding knuckles had become independent beings and as if the raw scraping they had taken from the windowsill had been a way of preparing myself for an end to illusion. For better or worse, life now would have to be lived not inside an overheated imagination but in those harsh streets below the living room window. To speak of rage and anger as having ushered me into manhood may seem anachronistic. Yet that street below my window was one of the streets through which I would have to make my way if I wanted to claim a self from this encounter with anger—even if

I had to make my way through it on long-legged braces and crutches.

In the years that followed, I would begin to understand how much I owed to that cathartic explosion that picked me up and hurled me into my fear. More than any other moment in my life, that morning shaped my future, fed me the rhythms of all I would seek in the years to come. More than religion, more than childish fantasies of power and glory (which until that moment I managed to call up at will), anger purged me of the terror that I would acquiesce to the future the virus wanted to define for me. Anger taught me that I could still make demands upon mind and body, that to be a cripple did not mean that one was relieved of the obligation to be a man. If anything, to be a cripple meant that the need to be a man was stronger and even more decisive. It was a cathartic explosion of heart and mind in which the sense of one's own victimhood stood at the borders of true selfhood, awaiting the moment I could announce that I was what I had struggled to be. To feel such anger at one's proscribed fate was to demand justice for the self, to be accountable for the future one had to live, even as a cripple. That was its immense promise. And I seized it.

Anger is its own motivation. No other emotion, not even love, has pledged me gifts of greater value. I try to remind myself of that whenever I hear it spoken of as a "blinding" emotion, an unintentionally accurate word if applied to what I felt on that morning. Even blind anger is not necessarily negative. It can give a man the focus he needs. My anger that morning was a wound that was finally cleansed. A cripple was as responsible for his own life as anyone else—and the world awaited one, with or without legs.

An Emersonianism on the cheap? No doubt, it is. Why shouldn't it be? Anger fed the joy of the life that followed that knuckle-scraped outburst. Anger made me understand that the determination to get even with "my virus" was not as crazy as it sounded. Better to seek revenge than to acquiesce in one's own death. Better to struggle against an organism personified by rage than to reach passively for the fantasies of *Captain from Castille*. Anger taught me those lessons, bequeathing me a moment that led to even richer moments, filled not with anger but with a sense of accomplishment—even, at times, a sense of peace. Give anger its due. It cannot always be "constructive," but confronting the world with its honesty is true power. The gift is not the emotion but the honesty one takes from it, the sense of release that first overwhelms and then purges body and soul. That was what I felt after I pounded the window sill with my fists. And that is what I shall continue to cherish. We are, after all, told that we have no choice but to take death as we find it. Well, why not take life that way, too? Maybe anger really is our least primitive state.

Anger would not only motivate me; it would liberate me. There were times, I admit, when it grew so excessive that it crippled this cripple's ability to act in his own interest. For the most part, however, anger allowed me both a clarity of vision and a sense of purpose that kept the enemy visible, definable. It was fairly easy to keep from being burned out by anger. Even so unwieldy an emotion still takes the measure of one's need and aspiration. That failed poet now understands not only why anger is man's least primitive state but why he never threw his poems away. It takes nerve to stand an emotion on its head. "Compensation," Emerson called it. A timid man, Emerson, with a brave way of putting things. *Compensation* is as good a word as any to describe the gift of life that anger allowed me to seize for my own. And now, all these years later, the memory of its generosity urges me to offer others these few kind words for anger.

PART II

INTERLUDE: MYTH

4

BODILY
PASSIONS:

HEPHAESTUS AMONG THE GODS

*But my son Hephaestus whom I bore was weakly among all the
blessed gods and shriveled of foot, a shame and a disgrace to me
in heaven, whom I myself took in my hands and cast out so that
he fell in the great sea.*

Homeric Hymn to Hera

HERE THE BODY is text, a cuneiform of angles and jagged
edges, cut to the limping grace of its subject. Yet the subject himself leaves us edgy, caught as he is between the role of buffoon
and his desire to see himself as a true immortal, a divine warrior,
like his nemesis, Ares. On the frieze of the Parthenon, we see
him posed as a powerful muscular figure. The Phrynos Painter
depicts him in the act of splitting open Zeus' head so that
Athena can emerge fully formed into the world. And in all the
other images of Hephaestus we possess, he looks like any other
Greek god. Yet in all the myths that tell his story, he is singular,
a divinity held victim by a body that irritates him as much as it
irritates us. We expect a god to shroud himself in mystery, but

in Hephaestus we see the longings of a divinity forced to accommodate himself to physical imperfection. Immortal though he is, Hephaestus resembles mortal cripples in the most essential aspect of their lives—he is trapped within his own body, a god in whom divinity must float like a soap bubble between shadow and reality.

That a god's existence should be structured around bodily imperfections is bound to disturb a mere mortal, particularly those of us condemned to our own bodily anguish. The greatest artisan in Olympus is forced to humble himself, over and over again, by the reality of his puny, shriveled legs. To be an immortal and yet be forced to beg for the perfection that should belong to a god by right of birth cannot be easy. Gods are not supposed to be cripples. Most mortals view being crippled as a misfortune that simply happens to some people. There are those who have the luck of the draw and those who don't, and none of us can do very much about that. Only we expect a god to transcend a cripple's broken body.

Even a man like me, who possesses his own considerable stake in the story of the divine cripple, knows that he cannot demand justice from a universe more capricious than it is unjust, more dense than it is blind. Why, then, am I fascinated by and resentful of the fate imposed on Hephaestus? Why do I urge the divine smith to rise above the physical battles that plague my own life? Is it that I find a myth in which the physical body rules over a god as firmly as it rules over me perverse? I think of my body as a tough relentless jailer. For more than fifty years, that is how I have looked at it. Why shouldn't the body of a god twist in the wind, too? If he and I are truly joined as cripples, that alone is reason enough to acknowledge him.

Only the bond that binds us is not suffering but our knowledge of what the body is unable to do. Limitation is an irremediable fact of life. While I can resign myself to that easily enough, limitation in a god angers me. It's difficult to take, one of those psychological oxymorons for which there is no adequate explanation. A god who can fly like the wind through Olympus yet cannot stroll its streets as other gods do! A god who is the butt of *their* laughter, who is envious of their unbroken bodies! A god forced to limp through those divine alleys in search of his proper portion! Yet grudgingly, angrily, I limp alongside him in my imagination, searching for my own portion in his example.

For we are locked into our bodily aspirations, that crippled god and I, each of us an onlooker at the feast of life, each of us raging against the assumptions normal men make. We share a hunger for what the broken body will never possess. Do I care that no man can call his body his true home? ("Nor any god either!" the divine smith whispers in my ear, voice coated with an Olympian's disgust.) Does it matter that the body I yet dream of is not the body normal men live with? Even as an object of speculation and fantasy, the body is a source of blood, tears, and thwarted expectations.

What haunts Hephaestus haunts every cripple. Those with normal bodies can ignore the rage a cripple feels against everything in life he has not been allowed to experience. Ask me what I want and I will speak of a body that exists in the depths of my fantasies. Like the crippled god, I have never been able to accept what I was offered as my portion in life, even if that means dooming myself to the envy one sees in aging body builders who hang around gyms and talk of muscle mass and reps, eavesdropping on the childish catechisms of the young in the service of their own still-adolescent dreams. Like Hephaestus, like me, they, too, hunger for the unbroken body.

And why not? Socrates tells us that age should take a man beyond his bodily passions—evidence, if any were needed, that I am no Socrates, just another mortal trying to feed his desire to deny what happened to his own body more than fifty years ago. Health freezes in memory, but in life both the crippled god and I are left with token legs—withered, atrophied, dead to all but desire. It doesn't help to remind me that all bodies decay. After all, Hephaestus is immortal. Yet he still suffers envy. His immortality is not the source of his bodily anguish nor is it the solution to that anguish. Immortals may be able to ignore the part of the equation that speaks of death, yet the crippled god recognizes that the text is never of body alone. What haunts him is what haunts all cripples, that counter-body floating in the chambers of the mind, a visionary Platonic promise which we so desperately hunger to make real.

With Hephaestus, we begin on the following note: He is a cripple, a god, and the greatest artisan in Olympus. Lame and halt, he limps through the domain of his father Zeus with as little grace as Dickens allows the unctuous Tiny Tim, who is carried like a sack of potatoes on his father's shoulders through the dank streets and back alleys of Victorian London. Hephaestus needs no mirror to see what his withered legs look like. God or mortal, a cripple is a cripple. Nor does he need keen ears to listen to the mocking laughter of his fellow gods. There are powers that no cripple, god or man, can possess. In Greek myth, Hephaestus is usually depicted as a god with a gentle disposition. But in my mind, he exists in a rage of humiliation, another cripple seeking to get even with his fate.

The universe has laws and rules, even for immortals. Should Hephaestus expect not to be cuckolded because he gives himself over to dreams of the flesh? He loves his wife, the beautiful Aphrodite, with envy, passion, and longing. That she toys with him by allowing Ares to make love to her in the bed she has shared with him is of less consequence than the spectacle he makes of himself when he traps his wife in the arms of her lover. Did he intend to illustrate his skill in the art of entrapment? Does he expect us to admire the invisible net he made and then cast over Aphrodite and Ares asleep on the bed? Even in revenge, this god is clownish and awkward. What does he gain by chaining the two faithless lovers to the bed? Distance from a too-sexy wife? Or is he just made to appear even more of a buffoon, when Aphrodite, still in the throes of her ardor, proves so tempting a vision to the other gods that she sends them to the keyhole of their own desire—divine voyeurs all, immortal peeping Toms?

It is Aphrodite's revenge, not Hephaestus', that we are forced to recognize. For him, this is just another humiliation, like his failed rape of Athena. Aphrodite knows that, even when bungled, passion speaks to the beauty it woos. Yet say this for our lame smith—his courage as lover reaches beyond his grasp. He loves where he has no prospect of success. Married to the most self-absorbed of goddesses, the word made into a flesh artists will paint and poets will praise, he clings to her beauty as if love were his to bestow. What can be braver than a lover who risks humiliation at his beloved's hands? Like so many cripples, Hephaestus loves the bodily perfection denied him.

Hephaestus possesses a plodding integrity, and his insistence on going his own way gives him genuine appeal. But he is the victim of his needs. Even a god's courage is not blind. He senses what will happen if he insists upon the legitimacy of his own bodily hungers. Yet he insists—and goes to his cuckoldry, a limping divinity playing with a fire more searing than that of the forge on which he molds the shield of Achilles. He limps to the bitter music of his fellow gods' mocking laughter. Nonetheless, his endurance wins our admiration even as it evokes our envy.

For he is not a willing victim. And that is what saves him. If Greek myth possesses a single god who has the virtues of a peasant, Hephaestus is that god. Central to his story is his skill as an artisan. The fact that he is a maker of useful objects, along with the fact that he is crippled, is all we truly know about him. Yet the god of craftsmen must limp to his forge on the shoulders of the two golden mechanical statues he creates to help him walk (if only he had cast Aphrodite as so willing a helpmate), a magician of fire and metal. Both his limp and his need for the help of his golden statues make him seem more of a god-like mortal than a true god. Can talent alone still serve him in an age that confuses the divine with the sensational? Like Kazantzakis' Christ, modern man defines his faith in the divine through the persistence of his doubt in his own singularity. His gifts rarely satisfy his needs. Despite his talent as an artisan, the true nature of divinity eludes Hephaestus. He will never be able to transform his own broken body into one of his beautiful and useful objects.

Limping cuckold, singed Cellini of the heavens, craftsman burdened by his love of Aphrodite, he is a naif, as innocent a lover as he is a skilled artisan. Generous and crotchety, he willingly gives of his talent as a maker of things. He demonstrates that gods, like men, must sometimes embrace lives they do not want. One envisions him standing before Zeus, pride and defiance displayed in his face. Can an immortal woo Aphrodite without being made aware of what he must pay for the risk of love? Like the mortal men and women they crush, the gods, too, must struggle for primacy—Zeus and Hera, Apollo and Artemis, Hephaestus and Aphrodite. His limp defines Hephaestus as a crippled artisan; it also defines his limitations as a god.

Hesiod mockingly called Hephaestus "the famous cripple," as if the fact that he was both divine and lame was enough to make us aware of the absurdity ruling the universe. The contradictions imposed upon his body speak of conflicts that he alone, among all the Olympians, is forced to live with. In the standard version of the myth, Hephaestus is crippled by his own mother. Repulsed by his ugliness, Hera hurls him into the sea, a maternal act perverse enough even for an age weaned on Freud and Hitchcock. Enraged by her son's inability to flatter her needs, Hera is willing to make him bait for Poseidon's fish. But he is rescued by the sea nymphs, Thetis and Euryonome, who take him to their underwater grotto. Here he learns the smith's craft and begins to brood over his broken body. Here, too, he first seeks to impose his imperfect presence upon the normal world.

In an alternative version of his creation myth, Hephaestus chooses the side of his mother against his father, Zeus. Like a gang leader trapped by the oaths he must swear for the sake of his position, he must either follow through or lose face. Zeus is so enraged at his son's disloyalty that he hurls him from the Olympian heavens to the island of Lemnos. Broken in body, shattered by his father's wrath, Hephaestus is stripped not merely of dignity (never a long suit in Greek myth) but of function, too. Nursed back to health by the mortals who live on Lemnos, human kindness proves to be his salvation. Here the myth is highly contemporary, as if we are being told that, in the mortal world, the crippled god is just another victim, human in need, broken in body, forced to measure himself against those who see him as the ultimate outsider.

To be ignorant of Greek myth, once unthinkable among the educated, is acceptable enough in an age of CNN and virtual reality. Given our insatiable appetite for stories of psychological significance, the face that launched a thousand ships now fondles its own image. Think of a winking Marilyn Monroe seeking to become simple Norma Jean again. When confronted with the anger of Hephaestus, we wonder whether he is merely a mortal in disguise, his psyche stained by his bodily defects. Is he to live meekly among gods who embody the perfection of physical form? Or is the day to come when he finds the vengeance he seeks?

It is not the god of whom we ask such questions, but the cripple. For the cripple is distinguished by the absence of the symmetry and physical beauty that the other Greek gods possess. Yet it is Hephaestus who enriches the other gods by placing his remarkable skills at the service of their pleasure. With a sense of craftsmanship as powerful as fire and as delicate as fog, he works his work. Not even Zeus provides such splendid gifts to gods and men. Yet his is not the kind of divinity that teaches mankind useful lessons. Sisyphus pushing his rock to the top of a mountain, doomed to repeat the act perpetually, is the myth that Camus made into the spiritual guidon of a generation bloodied by totalitarianism and the horrors of World War II. But Camus' myth seems too consciously literary today, like Dostoevsky's insistence that hell is merely the absence of love. In the world after Auschwitz, love's absence, like a toothache, wears us down. What we seek is not love but justice. The suffering of Hephaestus humanizes us, for the struggles of this cripple resemble our struggles far more than does the ordeal of Sisyphus.

Hephaestus is not an intellectual. He is neither writer nor philosopher. "I suffer for you," Malamud's world-weary grocer says to his assistant when asked why Jews suffer. A belief in liberation through suffering remains endemic to most religions, and it seems natural for a Morris Bober to mortgage his existence to the idea of suffering as a good. The ancient Greeks were more matter of fact about suffering. To suffer was, as the Chorus says in Sophocles' *Oedipus Rex*, "man's inexorable fate." But it was no more than that. What mattered for an Athenian in the fifth century B.C. was not individual suffering but the courage with which men handled suffering. And courage is the word for what Hephaestus offers us. His behavior in the face of his bodily humiliation is not only courageous but human. He endures what men must endure simply because they are mortal.

For the ancient Greeks, one of the functions of divinity was to reflect how cruel ordinary life is. Hephaestus understands that his broken body exists as the center of its own universe. Like Shakespeare's Richard III, he sees himself as "unfinished" and "incomplete." But where Shakespeare's king struggles with his bodily imperfections until he transforms himself into a man feeding off all that stands in his way, so swollen with his sense of humiliation that he is blind to all else, Hephaestus seeks revenge on fate by imposing shape on matter. Richard plots murder after murder, scheming to hold on to crown and power. Hephaestus, smoldering with rage, creates the shield of Achilles.

"Why is Hephaestus . . . a cripple?" asks G. S. Kirk in his excellent book, *The Nature of Greek Myths*. A scholarly question, it demands a personal answer of those who are themselves crippled. Hephaestus is a cripple because cripples existed in the Greek world as they do in ours; he is a cripple because Greek myth was set down by a blind poet; he is a cripple because Greek myth could celebrate a club-footed king who solved riddles. Professor Kirk understood our need to make Greek myth relevant. There may be better stories to illustrate how courage is needed to defy fate; there are certainly more contemporary ones. But the myth of Hephaestus disturbs us because he is the only crippled god we have.

It is important to remind ourselves that Greek myth was

never intended as dogma but as stories hinting at how order was imposed upon a chaotic universe. Like all myth, it embraced the desire to understand human nature as well as the desire to understand the natural world. On some level, every myth is about how unexplainable and inscrutable existence is. Like so many ancient stories, the myth of the crippled god is as important for what it reveals about its culture as for what it tells us about Hephaestus. What we take from it is bound to be different from what an Athenian took from it five centuries before the birth of Christ. Our response to that ancient story is bound to be far more individualistic than it is collective.

Yet we must respond if the myths are to continue to speak to us. I read the story of Hephaestus as the story of a fellow cripple. But I also read the story as a modern man doomed to live with knowledge that leads not to certainty but to growing doubt about the meaning of life. In the figure of Hephaestus, I discover a tough-mindedness that I myself need to triumph over the twin temptations of total rage and/or mawkish self-pity. A man forced to live with what his body has surrendered learns how important it is to push himself beyond bitterness and cynicism. Sooner or later, he must face the consequences of loss and disease honestly. From my perspective, Hephaestus is a cripple because he was created not *in* my image but *for* my image at a time when both gods and men believed that life was to be faced with courage. That courage seems to have been dropped from our list of virtues does not take away from its reality. The willingness to endure is what any cripple who chooses to live among the normals of this world needs. The myth of Hephaestus speaks to me of what it means to be an outcast. And like all myths transposed to modern times, it demands a deeply personal response.

When I began teaching in the 1960s, college sophomores were expected to read Tennyson's great poem, "Ulysses." The poet depicts the Greek warrior as an aging king contemplating his youthful adventures. Tired of a dutiful son, bored by a scolding wife, he despairs of a life in which he must "mete and dole unequal laws unto a savage race." Telemachus and Penelope are embodiments of order and propriety. Because he rules over a land where form breeds manners, Ulysses wants to set out again for unknown seas and embattled shores—and to take along his old comrades who fought with him before the gates of Troy.

"Ulysses" was a widely anthologized poem well into the 1970s, when it became a casualty of the growing demand for "relevance," a curious fate for a poem that addresses contemporary problems far more truthfully than almost any recent poem I can think of. In an essential Victorian text, Tennyson conceives of the good life in an aging warrior's determination to make himself once again part of "one equal temper of heroic hearts." The need for physical courage was a staple of Victorian thought, although the poem is usually read as a paean to intellectual curiosity. Yet "Ulysses" is as much about the body's need to confirm itself through struggle as about intellectual exploration. Ulysses cannot accept the physical failures of aging. He remains alert to life's promise even as his body betrays the past. He wants to confront the known and unknown as he once did, yet he recognizes the physical limitations age insists on. Only in action can he face the prospect of ending life with dignity. Mortality demands the dignity of resistance, while courage lies in facing the imminence of death. The poem allows for the inevitable decline of body and mind, while affirming the traditional idea that the test of a man is how he manages that decline.

The Greeks were fortunate in their choice of gods. Divinities who make human frailty palatable by making weakness the property of god and man allowed them to think they were part of an order that, if violent, was also natural. In a first-rate study of Vietnam veterans afflicted with post-traumatic stress disorder, *Achilles in Vietnam*, the psychiatrist Jonathan Shay compares the traumatized down-and-out derelicts he treats in and around Boston to the warriors, both Greek and Trojan, Homer writes about. That the Homeric gods reflected human failings and human temptations was noted long before Dr. Shay pointed to Zeus' "casual indifference" to suffering. The gods switch allegiance from one side to another and alternate between bored indifference and passionate involvement. But Shay's study eliminates time as a barrier to the understanding of myth. Zeus allows himself to be seduced by Hera in the midst of a bloody battle between Greek and Trojan, yet he can speak compassionately of the fallen warriors on both sides in a scene that is mockingly contemporary.

To the modern sensibility, the Greek gods are not so much paradoxical as erratic. They resemble us—as petulant as Achilles, as self-righteous as Menelaus—much more than the Hebrew Yahweh does, except for their immortality. H. D. F. Kitto called the gods "sublimated Kings," human in all but the length of their days. Yet no Greek god is human in the sense that Christ is human. The agony of Hephaestus has nothing to do with the idea of sacrificing one's divine body for the sake of mankind. The pain he feels is the pain of *his* body, and he suffers that pain for his own sake. Unlike Malamud's Jewish grocer, he endures and suffers for the self alone. If his suffering is profound, he is ordinary. Despite Hephaestus' status as god-artisan, he is like us in his desire to make sense out of the senselessness of his fate.

Gods who lie and cheat and steal and drink experience the very same passions that imprison the mortals they lord it over. They are deceitful and bawdy and childish; they practice sexual blackmail; they know the lessons of humanity. Yet no god is compelled to become human, which may help explain why

Hephaestus' faults endear him to us. We struggle for the kind of courage he possesses. His anguish stems from his bodily failures, and we see what he has paid for his endurance as he struggles against physical limitation. Gods, like men, shrink from the prospect of pain—for pain not only hurts, it humiliates.

Hephaestus' position in the pantheon is that of the most put upon of immortals. He is plodding, he lacks a sense of the dramatic, and, except for his attempted rape of Athena, he is not really a creature of excess—and excess is what we expect of gods. His life is symbolized by that incongruous limp. A god who is crippled violates our sense of natural order, yet he is the god who commands respect for his insistence on facing a destiny as comic as it is painful. Plagued by everything that plagues humanity, he confronts the same enemies any mortal cripple must confront. His possibilities and his limits are defined by others— Zeus, his fellow gods (all of whom find his lameness comic), Homer, Hesiod.

Only his endurance is beyond their control. Our gimpy-legged smith is as good an example as we possess of the groping courage that defines man at his most resistant. While his power is no match for the power of a Zeus or a Hera, he resists the limits they try to impose upon him. Despite his promiscuous wife, despite a father and mother prepared to keep him in his place, life remains his to define. As a god, he must answer to Zeus. As an artisan, he must answer to the needs of others. But as the model of what a man can create out of his own pain, he speaks directly to us. The endurance of this limping god at his bellows is an example that can be followed even beyond Olympus.

That his talent as an artisan is linked to his loneliness binds Hephaestus to us. To know that the parts of the body must com-

pensate for what the whole body can no longer do is to know the
contradictions cripples must live with. God or man, every cripple is by definition Emersonian *manque*. We pay for our lessons
in pain and humiliation with a compensation that ordinary men
and women cannot dream of. A normal seeking to know the
price of physical affliction could do worse than envision our
crippled smith's powerful arms and chest and shoulders, noting
how awkwardly he moves, how his childish steps lack grace and
surety. Listen to him mocked by those who view that powerful
torso, set like a shaky vase on a rickety table, as divine slapstick
in the making. Feet twisted, legs atrophied—in a symmetry of
broken parts, he limps among us, cripple and god, Quasimodo
with a dislocated hip. Gait stolen from a Chaplinesque sailor or
a Jerry Lewis "spastic" before Lewis turned himself into a telethon barker for those he now unctuously calls "my kids," his
bodily presence is as laughable as it is heroic. Weaving into our
mockery, a cripple pushing past the physical perfection claimed
by the other Olympians, broken and twisted, he is, strangely
enough, the most buoyant of the gods. Like aging Ulysses, he demands the risk of our emulation.

My affection for Hephaestus has to do not with his talent but
with his defiance. Maybe I admire him beyond his actual worth,
as I admire Beckett and Kafka, who set examples of literary courage for other writers—the same kind of courage that sends
Hephaestus to his forge to build palaces for those who mock
him, to create the golden throne of a father who hurls him bodily
from the heights of Olympus. Do we merely praise what he creates? Or do we use his example to allow our own imperfections
honestly to occupy center stage?

In one of his best essays, Edmund Wilson speaks of another
Greek myth, that of Philoctetes, as "a parable of human charac-

ter" which clarifies the artist's ambiguous relationship to the
world. Only after Philoctetes cleanses his fellow Greeks
through his wound and magic bow can the Trojans be defeated.
Like Hephaestus' limp, Philoctetes' wound sets him apart. The
modern reader has to wonder how, alone on his deserted island,
Philoctetes understood the myth of Hephaestus. As an example
of defiance and endurance? Or as the story of a god enraged by a
dream of vengeance? Not even the ability to create placates men
housed in bodies in which extremes of weakness and determination wrestle for possession of the spirit.

Hephaestus is no Stephen Hawking, prepared to explore the
body of time by defying the body of a cripple. Yet being crippled
defines his place on Olympus more than his talent does. Trapped
by legs unable to do what legs are supposed to do, laughed at,
scorned, Hephaestus offers us the work of his hands. He may
worship his promiscuous wife's perfect body, but he is a god
whose life is ruled by his own substantial talent as a smith If his
body is not what he would have chosen, it is still *his*, an Olympian body. And that leads to the final paradox Hephaestus must
live with—that he, a crippled god, is to become the god of striv-
ing cripples. The most physical of Greek divinities, he stands,
legs shaky and weak, alone with his body, stranger on Olympus.

"I wouldn't want to put my money on a cripple." The dialogue is
not from *The Iliad* but from Robert Rossen's film noir classic,
The Hustler. And the speaker is not Zeus or Hera or the promiscuous Aphrodite but George C. Scott in the role of the gambler-
fixer. Scott's words are directed at Fast Eddie, a pool room hustler played by Paul Newman. And the cripple on whom Scott
will not put his money is Piper Laurie, a wealthy, intellectual
college girl who limps into the life of the hustler. Newman
frowns, glances at his damaged girl friend, and objects to the use

of the word "cripple." Even as far back as 1961, Hollywood was eager to seem politically correct.

"A fact is a fact," pipes up Piper, a moment of particular lucidity for a woman drinking herself to sex and suicide. As limps go, Piper's is not much. Hollywood could never allow a mere limp to lessen the allure of a whiskey-battered but still-sexy body. Yet her limp is the significant aspect of her character, the single identifiable trait with which she herself defines hope and despair. And it is her only weapon in the struggle with the gambler for Fast Eddie's grungy working-class soul. Eddie is able to resist the allure of a sexy body, but the limp brings out the would-be savior in him. Every victim has needs. And in *The Hustler*, even the jaded gambler is a victim. The lady with the limp wins the battle by losing the war. She liberates the poolroom hustler from his own mercenary nihilism, but at the price of her own extinction.

An immortal cannot commit suicide. Hephaestus is a god, while poor Piper is a lady who limps, in love with a handsome poolroom hustler. She is also more pitiful than our crippled god. Hephaestus does not need to offer his pain as a sacrifice to enable normals to beg forgiveness for being straight of limb and bone. He has no interest in shaming us by making us remember the less fortunate. His endurance provokes us, for it is raw enough to make us feel shame.

It is impossible to separate the courage of this god from his limp, for the limp reminds us, as it reminds him, that a Zeus or a Hera is always waiting, demanding submission, ready to hurl their disobedient son to Lemnos or the sea. Yet even as Hephaestus holds to the model of Kafka, forced himself to endure the power of the father, his dream of an unscarred body betrays him. Aphrodite makes him a cuckold, and he discovers that a god, too, must pay for desire. It is the crippled god, not the limping woman, who stands by bodily passion. Braced by mechanical statues, ready for the blows of Zeus or the vanity of Hera or the mocking laughter of his fellow Olympians, he works—and endures.

During a time in which the Homeric world is viewed as just another realm of the dead white males of Western culture, we should not be surprised that the courage the lame god displays, the courage of the body that refuses to accept the portion fate allots to it, does not count for much. We live, after all, in a nation in which bodies are merely interchangeable parts. The source of Hephaestus' courage is the will that allows him to push his body beyond itself, to challenge and resist its limitations. Condemned to envy of the normal gods, he may dream of violence, but he knows that he needs more than violence to survive: he needs courage.

"It's not enough that you just have talent. You gotta have character, too," the embittered hustler tells the gambler-fixer after his crippled girl friend's suicide gives him the courage for life she lacked. On the verge of beating Minnesota Fats and making his mark as premier poolroom hustler in the land, he offers that small philosophical crumb. However banal, it is true. While the cripple pays the price, the hustler eats the candy. Portentous and heavy-handed, it is the kind of advice that suits a culture fed its myths by Hollywood. Yet I prefer the Greek god, who tells us to get even with fate by denying the sentimental obligations it insists we accept. Unlike Piper, Hephaestus earns his limp, as he earns his rage against the body that betrays him. His courage is beyond myth. Plodding, repetitive, as dull as exercise, it has become a habit, the way his body must resist its unjust fate.

Dr. Shay found little to choose between those who fought before the walls of Troy and those who fought in the rice paddies of Vietnam. Crippled by love or war or disease, men are defined by the fate they refuse as much as by the fate they are forced to accept. Like Hephaestus, we endure the mixture of weakness and strength that is what we mean by the word "character." None of us can claim courage as a permanent possession, yet each of us, like the crippled smith urging himself to bodily defiance, must give himself over to the demands of his singular struggle. That example is worth following. And so I watch the lame god push his body through the heavens of Olympus, and my own cripple's heart fills with envy of and admiration for this brother in the kingdom of the crippled, my shining example of the will to endure.

PART III

ICONS
AND IMAGES

5

BEACHES
IN WINTER

WE KNOW our dreams as we know our weaknesses, each of them catching us in the soft familiarity of acceptance. Only the acceptance of dreams must not be confused with self-indulgence, a warning that explains, as much as anything can, why I no longer find dreaming of beaches threatening. For even in my dreams, those beaches have become soothing places, quietly pedestrian in the familiarity of their appeal. And why not? Long stretches of sand were never intended to force passion from the soul or to plague the introspective will with reminders of all the work one has left undone. It would be difficult for any writer to transform a dream of beaches into the kind of sordid confession we enjoy offering the world, voices nervous and hesitant, as if words might unintentionally reveal the crazed Poe gnawing away at the soul's inner anguish.

With beaches, it's enough to begin with the observation that they really are pedestrian places. And yet, I still dream of them—as if pedestrian places merit no better than pedestrian dreams. Admittedly, I am old enough now so that I do not need dreams of insatiable sexual appetite being satisfied or exotic adventures that take one to strange places. The dreams of adolescence are almost certain to bore anyone who is no longer an adolescent. By the time a man hits thirty, his dreams probably should tend toward a certain parochialism. The lines of sun and sand that I dream of form a maze for the reflective imagination—and a quiet maze at that, a labyrinth in which form is usually drama enough.

At best, dreaming of beaches offers nothing better than a drift into the familiar. Beaches do not threaten us. On the beach, a man serves as pleasure's attendant—not the most taxing of roles. Even in the space that beaches occupy in my imagination, they tend to be tranquil places. Dreaming of them does not hint at forebodings of tragedy or some impending catastrophe about to swallow up life the second one wakes in terror to grasp at the relief offered by, "It's only a dream." The average man or woman looks at a beach and discovers a meditative quiet, an introduction to surfaces that flatten out complexity's curves. To dream of beaches is to feel a quiet satisfaction with the world as it is.

I have been dreaming of beaches for twenty-eight years, and I expect to continue dreaming of them until the day I die. As dreams go, the prospect is not particularly disturbing. Envision a sparkling plane of ocean, soft waves serenely lapping against sloping white sands: not an image to intimidate man or woman. Dreaming of beaches allows for emotion recollected in tranquillity, the core, as Wordsworth says, of true poetry. And I am now at that stage in my own life where I prefer quiet contemplation to the rage and sense of loss my more violent dreams used to arouse in me.

Dreaming of beaches, I feel neither envy nor animosity. In my dreams I am not particularly dissatisfied with my lot in life, nor do I find myself angry at a world that does not behave as I think it should. Dreaming of beaches does not ask me to be concerned about the homeless or force me to think about AIDS or what I can do to lessen the tension between blacks and whites in New York City or the ways this America I love has learned of late to stick it to the poor and helpless. Neither the demands of my own ego nor my obligations to the egos of others concern me when I dream of beaches. It is the play of light on water that concerns me, the dance of days whipped by wind. Fog and cloud and mist and the smell of an impending storm concern me. Like the prospect of retirement, a beach forces a man to focus on what lies beyond, to squeeze understanding from observations that once seemed casual and innocent but are suddenly revealed to be the essence of what life offers.

I am writing these sentences about beaches while sitting at a Parsons table which currently serves as my desk, in an apartment overlooking a long stretch of gray sand in the South Carolina Low Country. I have come here to get away from the rawness of New York in winter and to begin work on a new novel. At least, that is why I tell myself I have come here. I suspect that what I have actually come for is to do what I am doing at this precise moment—gazing out at the splendid beach below my window in the ceaseless effort to fortify my spirit.

It is a week before Christmas and I am now watching a lone man wearing a blue windbreaker take long strides across the sand. A big gray dog lopes at his heels, occasionally darting ahead and then playfully circling back, raising its head and barking in anticipation of its owner's approval. The man and dog share the soft familiarity of the beach, a loose equality of motion which allows them both to move with grace toward their destination. The scene is casual—yet it is precise and sharp and decisive. And it embodies a certain perfection of form: space, sand, the movement of man and dog. It is seven twenty-five in the morning and I have been sitting at this table since five-thirty. First, I saw the break of light that indicates sunrise, and then I watched as a dark horizon gave way to an ocean so flat and soothing I could scarcely tell where the sand ended and the water began. This beach on a winter morning has drained me of the burdens of the self. Watching the man and his dog move across the sand, I feel extraordinarily happy. I feel prepared for the day ahead.

On the line of horizon where ocean meets sky, two shrimp boats drift, methodically rousing themselves toward the near shore. In another hour, their gull-like riggings with the box traps that stir bottom water will slip around the long sand bar that juts at low tide a mile or so into the ocean. The boats will move toward shore, toward me, a hesitant wash of drift to tempt the moment with their slow, purposeful advance. For some unknown reason, the movement of these shrimp boats toward shore brings to mind images of burlesque dancers in Union City, New Jersey, women who tempted my adolescence as they tempted the adolescence of any number of Bronx boys in the 1950s. The images clot my mind, so quick and unexpected that they are embarrassing. Seeking to protect memory, I laugh.

Cautiously, the boats work in toward the shallows. I assume that the eyes of the shrimpers, like my own eyes, are focused on a flock of pelicans skimming the water directly in front of the boats. In flight, the pelicans look like formations of torpedo bombers in black and white movies about World War II. They fly side by side, in parallel groups of six. I expect them to peel off as if they were preparing to attack enemy ships. Along with the shrimp boats and the man and his dog and the raucous memory of burlesque strippers in Union City, those water-skimming pelicans feed my joy. Perched on dock posts, pelicans are extraordinarily ugly, primordial looking creatures. But as they fly into the horizon in rigorous yet fluid formation, they seem part of a pattern that has been set before me, a design from which nothing, not even silence, has been excluded.

On the television news from Beaufort last night, I heard a shrimp boat captain complain that the Low Country shrimp were smaller than in years past. The true source of his irritation turned out to be not the size of the shrimp caught off these coastal Carolina waters but the massive imports of shrimp from China which, he grumbled, were killing the trade. "In a few years, there won't be a shrimp boat left in the Low Country." Listening to him fills me with irritation, the way I often feel for my countrymen when I shop in the Food Lion on Palmetto Road and notice that the six cars lined up next to each other in the parking lot all have been made in Japan. My countrymen are selfish and my countrymen are taking a beating. This Carolina shrimper's anger echoes the Detroit auto worker's indignation at what CNN commentators persist in calling "free market forces."

But the sight of the man and his dog on the beach and the pelicans and shrimp boats moving across the ocean makes it difficult to focus on trade policy. When I think of beaches, politics and economics grow distant. What is important is watching the early morning sun enfold the sand of this Carolina coast in winter, the one season when beaches are absolutely true to their own nature. The sight of this beach makes me want to examine more cosmic issues than trade policy. A beach in winter is a bargain between a man and his God. Who wants to think of trade policy when the world seems so quietly alive? This beach in winter offers as much tranquillity as even Wordsworth might have wished for.

Curiously, it is only the beach in winter that shows up in my dreams. I have spent summers on Spain's Costa del Sol and on Cape Cod and Fire Island and on Long Island's Hamptons. Yet I cannot remember dreaming of those beaches in summer. The beaches I dream of are hard clear landscapes, their dream air soft yet sharp, the way the air is in mid-December here in the Carolina Low Country, the cutting edge of a bright diamond that will never scar. In my dreams, I never see myself sweating as I stroll along the beach. Nor must I apply lotion or cream to block the sun's rays from face and shoulders. In dreams, the beach is not so much a window on real life as it is an escape hatch. The beach is my alternative to all the getting and spending of ordinary life, an investment in a soft time that protects all those private moments a man feels privileged to have witnessed. And the beach is an affirmation of my own past—like the memory of Sal Maglie's stubble-darkened face caught by the camera as he wound up to throw a curve ball, or the way Ted Williams had of staring at the pitcher on that mound sixty feet away.

I am not the kind of man who looks for eternity in a grain of sand. Nor in a billion grains of sand. I accept the curves of the mind with as little resistance as I accept the curves of the universe. If that is the way it is, then that is the way it is. What choice do I have but to accept it? For me, beaches link space to space—sand to water, water to horizon. Their beauty is not what men bring to fruition. That is the beauty of music, of poetry, of the language of the human. Yet even in my dreams, the beauty of beaches denies a sense of preeminence to mankind. What's Mozart to those hundreds of gulls whom I see pirouetting into the sun, as if they were answering a casting call for Hitchcock's *The Birds*? This beach was not made for man; *La Nozze De Figaro* was.

I love mountains and cities as much as I love beaches. And I continue to feel an unbroken if sometimes bitter passion for the battered streets of New York City where I have lived most of my life. But I do not dream of mountains and I do not dream of those city streets. Of course, the action of a dream is sometimes scripted on mountains or on city streets. But locale is secondary to meaning. What is important in any man's dreams is the way the narrative line asserts itself—what, how, and why what happened had to happen. Let me confess that I haven't been in a New York subway for some thirty-two years. Yet I still ride the subway in my dreams, searching for that deus ex machina who will bring me from place to place, from scene to scene, from action to action.

William Jennings Bryan, that famed Boy Orator of the Platte, felt enough fundamentalist fervor as he was testifying at the Scopes Monkey Trial to sneer at the great counsel for the defense, Clarence Darrow. If evolutionists like Darrow wanted to waste their time hunting for Cain's wife, that was certainly their privilege. Bryan, however, wanted it known to one and all that he didn't particularly care who had been the mother of Cain's children. Any mystery good enough for the God of Genesis was good enough for William Jennings Bryan. In the same spirit, I invite others to decipher the significance of mountain or subway in my dreams. Only when it comes to dreaming of beaches, my message remains as sharp as it is hostile: you can keep your theories to yourself.

A good friend of mine once chanced my enmity by suggesting that perhaps the reason I dream of beaches is that they have made me physically uncomfortable ever since I lost the use of my legs. My irritation with him subsided when I mulled over what he had said and decided that my friend probably had a point. No matter how firm and well-packed a beach is, the fact is that crutches and wheelchairs sink in sand. That is simply the way it is. When I was a younger man and a mere fledgling as a cripple, I was fiercely determined to outmuscle fate. That was when I would force myself to walk across the grainy traps of Robert Moses's Orchard Beach in the Bronx on braces and crutches, a struggle I can only compare to swimming against a crashing surf, the heavy waves making the task exhausting. It can be done. But the price one pays can cripple even the dedicated cripple. It's one thing if a cripple occasionally tries to match his strength of character and will against that ocean of sand—but he has to possess hubris tempered by chutzpah if he intends to make such challenges a persistent habit. In the final analysis, all excessive effort denies significance to motion. The same goes for pushing a wheelchair over the sand. It can be done. Only it is exhausting, and makes you feel punch-drunk with the cost of your effort.

And for what? Loss is loss and one cannot explain the world merely from the scars loss leaves in its wake. The crippling effects of a polio virus made it equally impossible for me to climb mountains or to ski. Yet just as I do not dream of mountain-climbing, I do not dream of skiing either. It doesn't matter that I have driven through the Alps, have gotten through the mountains of Spain, Colorado, New Mexico, Utah, Oregon, Idaho, Canada. It doesn't matter that I love mountains and that, even today, I sometimes feel the urge to climb some jagged peak. It is one of the things I still wish I could have done. Nonetheless, I don't *dream* about those things. And that is a difference worth noting.

In the summer of 1977, my younger son climbed Mt. Saandia outside of Albuquerque with a friend of mine, an experienced hiker and climber. Bruce was ten at the time, tough for his age but very much a child of the city. I drove to the summit to greet him on his arrival at the top of the mountain. He arrived out of breath and quite obviously irritated. For he had not been convinced of why he was climbing the mountain. "Okay, I've done it," he said testily. "And I hope this gets it out of your system."

Such psychological precocity irritates more than it enlightens. A grown man in his late twenties now, Bruce still refuses to believe me when I insist that the desire to climb a mountain was never in my system. Not in the sense that he assumes it was. Mountains are beautiful, yes. But mountains don't intrude on the territory of my psyche. Of course, I would like to know what it feels like, but that is mere hunger for experience. I would like to know what it feels like to ride a rocket to the moon, too. Yet my dreams are of beaches in winter.

I cannot remember dreaming about beaches until 1964, a few months after my wife and I and our older son, then four months short of his second birthday, arrived in the Netherlands for a Fulbright year abroad. Housing was in very short supply in the Netherlands in 1964, and two weeks after our arrival we were still stuck in a hotel in the Hague, searching for a place to live. One afternoon we were driven to a seaside village between the Hague and Amsterdam. Noordwijk aan Zee housed fishermen and tulip growers in 1964, but its chief function for many years had been to serve as a summer resort for vacationers, the majority of them prosperous Germans. In 1964, the Germans already had been anointed as the economic kings of postwar Europe. And it was in their vacation terrain that we found an apartment facing the beach and the pounding surf of the North Sea.

I had never before lived with a view of beach and water. And I had never before been conscious of the surf pummeling the shore, the way I became a few weeks after we moved into that apartment in Noordwijk, when a two-day blow tore into the North Sea coast with truly awesome power. That North Sea beach was not as attractive as the beach I look down on in South Carolina or the splendid ocean beaches of New York's Fire Island. But there was something that seemed overwhelmingly seductive about the beach at Noordwijk, some presence that held me, face to the harsh wind, not wanting to surrender the glimpse into my soul that living with that view of sand and ocean offered.

For Harriet, the beach at Noordwijk was a spiritual sanctuary. Bundled like a Dutch *huisvrouw* in coat and heavy stockings, kerchief tied around her head as the thrust of wind slashed against her face, she used to go for long walks, alone or pushing the stroller of our two-year-old son in front of her. Perhaps because the Dutch were such stolid law-abiding people, Harriet would take particular delight every time she spotted the mast antenna of an illegal radio ship on the horizon—the Dutch had given it the wonderful Brechtian name of "Pirate Ship Veronica"—swaying in the wind like a drunk on the New York subway. For our son, Benjy, the beach was a huge sandbox that filled him with delight and more than a bit of apprehension. He loved the beach at Noordwijk, but he was also frightened of its capricious moods. After having romped with delight across the sand, he would quite suddenly back away from the ferocious pounding surf, testing not merely his limits but his sense of caution, too, as he acknowledged the incipient danger of a horizon so vast and distant that it threatened to scoop us all, mother, father, and Benjy himself, into oblivion.

That beach at Noordwijk was a stop sign for illusions. It forced me to acknowledge my own limitations. But it also soothed, as nature is expected to soothe us. One can respect courage, inculcate its demands like a disciplined diabetic giving himself an insulin shot. But sooner or later, one has to face the limitations of this mundane world's mundane demands. My dreams of beaches did not challenge those demands.

The beach at Noordwijk ran parallel to a concrete boulevard. Turn-of-the-century resort hotels and spas stood alongside each other like aging sentinels left over from a Europe long since dead but not yet altogether buried. These ornate wooden structures

seemed to have been lifted collectively from the thick pages of
Thomas Mann's imagination. (Mann, I discovered to my delight,
used to vacation in the large luxury hotel at the end of the boulevard, the Huis ter Duin, the most famous of the hotels that still
fronted the beach in Noordwijk in 1964. On this very beach,
Mann had written his splendid essay on *Anna Karenina* and
worked on a number of his finest stories.) The boulevard ran
about a mile from end to end. And I would walk it daily, my
crutch-kissed shoulders and brace-bound legs thrusting into a
wind that cracked at my body like a circus-master's whip. It
wasn't merely cold, that wind. New York winds can be just as
cold. And anyone who has braved the lake winds of Chicago
might scornfully think of those North Sea winds as mere practice runs. But there is something about the rawness of wind on a
beach in winter—and that northern European winter ran from
mid-October to the end of April—that plunges a man deep into
himself.

Sometimes, I would simply stand on that boulevard and watch
my wife walk on the beach, a figure growing smaller and smaller
as she moved south toward the dunes of Katwijk. At other times,
when Benjy decided he would rather walk with his father on the
boulevard than remain in the apartment with the young woman
who worked as our *huismeisje* or accompany his mother, he
would move alongside me, his fingers confidently curled around
the pinky of my right hand that jutted out from the crutch like a
cannibal's nose bone. Or I might stand alone, with neither wife
nor child, my eyes gratefully frozen to the sight of the waves
breaking against the beach, trying to insinuate myself into nature's good graces as I braced my body against that raucous wind.

None of this seems particularly dramatic. Why, then, was it in
Noordwijk that I first became a man who dreams of beaches? Is

it because the sands of that first beach I lived alongside made life richer and more challenging? Of course, I thought nothing of walking long distances on my braces and crutches back then. Yet will and determination and the power of forearms and shoulders were never quite sufficient to master the sand. I knew that. Nonetheless, I tried mastering it. I loved that beach at Noordwijk the way an old man loves the remembered image of a high-school sweetheart. Yet even as I loved it, I hated its coarse grittiness. A few miles up the road, the sand was hard and solid and as easy to walk on, even on crutches, as the beach at Daytona. On the beach at Zandvoort, the Dutch raced cars. On the beach at Noordwijk, horses and their riders splashed through the sand at low tide.

Whenever I tried to play with my son on the beach, my crutches would sink as if I were trying to move on quicksand. The beach at Noordwijk challenged my fatherhood. It denied my longing to be the American father I wanted to be. In my mind's eye, I used to throw my two-year-old son's legs across my shoulders, and, as he straddled my neck, my imagination would send me running like a blocking back straight against the oncoming waves. Or else I visualized myself walking across the sand with Harriet, pulling my wife against me, each of us part of the elements—earth, air, fire, water—even as we sought love's promise.

Curiously enough, though those fantasies remain so remarkably vivid, I no longer resent what I will never be able to do on a real beach. Crutches, I know, will sink in sand. And I know that I will never run with that two-year-old's legs straddling my shoulders (that two-year-old is now a man in his thirties), just as I will never walk on the beach with the woman I love. I will never slash against the open range of water. Nor will I ever stroll in the sharp light of a rising winter sun, dog at heel, as the pelicans skim the flat ocean that slips like silence against the sand. I will do none of these things. I will merely dream of doing them until the time comes when I can dream no more.

And yet, I can still hear—and I suspect I shall always hear—the dreamer in me demanding his right to run on that pristine winter beach. I can still hear the sound of wind and waves and the nervous giggle of that two-year-old straddled across my shoulders as he urges me on and on, into the crashing waves. And I know that deep within myself, I still want that dream made real. Just for once, a brief moment when the image becomes fact. Afterwards, I'll be content enough to settle for the lovely sight of this long stretch of sand in winter, knowing that I have work to do and that the vacation is over. Like me, the people have left—all of them, still dreaming of beaches in winter.

6

SUMMER
DREAMS

ON THE DAY they clinched the American League pennant at the end of September, 1945, every member of the Detroit Tigers baseball team signed an official American League ball to be sent to me in the upstate hospital where I was learning to live without the use of my legs. A few weeks earlier, my Uncle Moe had gone to Yankee Stadium to watch the Tigers, whom he always referred to as "the Detroits," play the New York Yankees. His seat was alongside the visitors' bullpen. In 1945, baseball was still a casual game, and it was much easier for fans to speak to ballplayers, particularly to the bullpen pitchers, who would loll in the sun until the call from the dugout came to warm up. My uncle spent some time that day talking about what he already called "my nephew's condition" to one of the pitchers taking the sun in the Tiger bullpen. The Yankees were not going anywhere during that final summer of wartime baseball, but the Tigers were locked in an exciting pennant race with the Washington Senators. If the Tigers went on to win the pennant, my uncle was assured by the pitcher (for reasons I do not fathom to this day, he refused to tell me which pitcher it was who made the promise), he would see to it that a baseball was signed, sealed, and sent to me at the New York State Reconstruction Home.

For my uncle, that baseball was a gift to his "sick" nephew; for the Tiger pitcher, now perhaps dead, it was probably a way of placating the baseball gods and ensuring a pennant for Detroit and a World Series share for himself. But for me, that ball became as pure an object of worship as any boy could conceive. No Percival or Galahad, purifying body and soul as he prepared to quest for the Holy Grail, could have held a piece of the true cross with the naked adoration with which I held that autographed ball in my hand.

Like every other boy in that hospital ward, each of us crippled by polio or arthritis or a disease that rotted the bones called osteomylitis, I was ordinarily generous with personal possessions. We boys shared books and comics and model airplanes as we shared pain and fear. But from the moment I removed it from its brown paper wrapper, that autographed baseball was set apart from the casual bartering of ward life. I kept it wrapped in orange cellophane in the top drawer of the night table next to my bed. While I was willing to show it to any boy who asked to see it, I alone had the right to touch it. The adoration of the boys in the ward was to come from the eyes alone—mine embraced fingers as well as eyes.

Not even my closest friends in the ward challenged my flagrant selfishness. That autographed baseball was somehow understood to be my personal talisman—and its promise was that my passion for the game would miraculously make me whole again. Those of my friends who shared my love of baseball must have sensed, as I did, that the Tigers of 1945 were a symbolically perfect team for a crippled twelve-year-old boy to worship. A club composed both of wartime misfits and splendid ballplayers, they had ridden the powerful bat of the great Hank

Greenberg—released from five years of army service early in August—and the talented arm of the stylish left-hander Hal Newhouser to take the pennant race from a stubborn Washington team by a game and a half.

The names on that ball constituted a litany of redemption for me. I still vividly remember the soothing effect silently reciting those names had whenever I removed the ball from its resting place in the nightstand drawer in the dark of night, enfolded by my close identification with Hank Greenberg (like me, a big right-handed hitter from the Bronx of Eastern European Jewish immigrant parentage), infused with the stubborn onomatopoeic burliness of Stubby Overmire's name, fascinated by the tongue-in-cheek excess of the name Dizzy Trout, inspired by the blocklike power of the big Cherokee Indian slugger, Rudy York.

A passionate Dodger fan, I would rather have met Pete Reiser than Hank Greenberg. But even at twelve, I understood that my worship of that baseball had nothing to do with individual players and even less to do with the ball's arrival in the ward the day after the Tigers defeated the Cubs in a thrilling if sloppily played World Series. Nor was it the subtlety of baseball as a game that made me touch that ball with the reverence a medieval mendicant must have felt as he touched the yellowed bones of a saint.

That ball simply embodied the idea of physical grace for me—a grace that had been ripped from my life by the virus more than a year earlier. I used to think that polio had merely reinforced my natural street skepticism. I was, after all, a child of a city where even five-year-olds pride themselves on the ability to accept the way things are. At twelve, I felt I should be able to face the prospects before me without illusion. Only I couldn't. Nor were any of the other boys in the ward, whether country-reared or city-bred, prepared to accept being crippled as a permanent condition. Even a twelve-year-old boy has to learn to work his way into the reality of absence. My lifeless legs might fail to respond to the ministrations of physical therapists, but in my mind I was still someday destined to play major league baseball.

Those names I recited perpetuated my illusion of becoming whole again. The great Greenberg had survived years of tank warfare. Prince Hal Newhouser pitched not only with exceptional skill but with a heart murmur serious enough to keep him out of the service. Doc Cramer treated my illusions and Skeeter Webb stung my still-potent aspirations and Jimmy Outlaw testified to the legitimacy of believing that a devious dreamer could play the role of cooperative patient.

When I returned to the city in August of 1946, I carried that autographed baseball with me. My books and comics and board games and model airplanes were left in the ward, to be distributed as the spoils of departure are usually distributed in hospitals and jails, random bequests as quixotic as disease mandated.

But once I settled again in the apartment in the Bronx where I lived with my mother and father and younger brother, the talismanic appeal of the baseball soon shriveled and died. No longer did I recite aloud those names etched across the yellowing horsehide and feel myself kissed by prospective redemption.

Not that I consciously faced the prospects of living out my life as a cripple. If anything, removed from a world in which everyone had been crippled, I felt the stigma of my situation even more. But I discovered that my imagination was capable of choosing other avenues of fantasy, and I learned to march in triumph to the beat of different drummers. At the corner candy store, I would purchase pulp magazines on which I gorged my craving for adventure and fantasy. On dead schoolday afternoons, when my normal friends were deciphering geometric codes and chemical balances in high school classrooms, I would drift over to the radio and tune into some afternoon radio soap opera probing the question of whether a woman could find romance after thirty-five. Long before I discovered Hemingway and Farrell and Wright and Mailer, I sought romance in the "historical" novels of Thomas B. Costain and Frank Yerby and Rafael Sabatini. And if I needed athletic fantasies, the voice of Red Barber describing the intricacies of Dodger baseball made my illusions more vivid, more specific, than merely reciting those names printed on an autographed baseball could possibly do.

But the game of baseball retained an imaginative purity I could not find elsewhere—not in pulp magazines, not in radio soap operas, not in popular fiction. Once I learned to maneuver up and down subway stairs and to walk long distances on braces and crutches, which came to seem as natural as shirt and pants, I would take the IND Line's D Train to Yankee Stadium to see a game in which perfection and subtlety had struck a singular balance. By the time I was fifteen, I recognized that not only would I never play baseball again but I would never again walk without braces strapped to my legs and crutches stabbing into my arms. And yet, such knowledge was accepted by my rational mind alone. My imaginative life sent me roaming through greener fields. The result was a kind of fantasized schizophrenia, a dual life in which, even as I forced myself to push on my braces and crutches through streets that threatened to hold me back, I would perform at bat and in the field with grace and skill, an adolescent dreamer, a player in whose passionate longing fantasy and reality were one and the same.

Curiously, no matter how strong my fantasies about again playing baseball became, my view of the game grew less romantic. Lovers become husbands and wives and fans become students of the game. And both the knowledge and the specific intimacies which they bring to what they feel so strongly about grow as if they possessed a life other than the life of the dreamer who calls them into existence.

And so I would drift back to catch a fly ball while listening to the soft southern timbres of Red Barber's voice, or else I would dance on my fantasy legs off third base, tutored by Jackie Robinson, threatening to steal home and bring the crowd in Ebbetts Field to its feet. Yet even as I dreamed of glory, I forced myself to concentrate on the task of rehabilitating myself. If I made a conscious choice to embrace fantasies of playing ball with a dreamer's skills, I unconsciously understood that the real me possessed a very damaged body and that my chances of survival in this world depended on how well I could learn to force that body to respond to its true needs.

I don't suppose the split between my imagination and the reality facing me was very different from what normal adolescents must live with. Desire outstrips performance for most sixteen- and seventeen-year-olds—and their fields of dreams lack even the icon ready to the touch I possessed. What they had was simply a more available sense of themselves as "normal." My adolescent friends knew what was expected of them. If their talents had failed to withstand the inevitable recognition age brings and they were forced to accept their limitations as athletes, they could still turn their attention to acceptable destinies. For me, on the other hand, illusion grew stronger and stronger precisely because there seemed to be so little beyond illusion.

I could only try to ignore the realities I could not control. If the major leagues beckoned in imagination, then braces and crutches could be ignored. I remained a ballplayer in my head, expecting that inevitable day when those braces and crutches would simply peel away, like the outer skin of an onion, and I would step through time and circumstance to recapture a boy's skill and prowess full-blown.

/ / /

A testament to the power of illusion, I forced myself to save my weekly allowance of fifty cents until I had enough money to purchase a first baseman's mitt. And I treasured that mitt, not as I treasured the autographed ball but because it fed my illusions in the most prosaic of ways. I oiled it lovingly, tying its clawlike halves around a baseball so that it would hold a shape designed to make me a fielder who possessed a sure glove.

I would lean against one of the cars parked on the street we lived on and have a catch with my younger brother or else with one of my friends. Abe and my friends were patient with me. They guarded my illusions, perhaps because their own had died. None of them would ever play major league baseball either, and if they had been called upon to serve as guardians of time's passing for me, well, then, they would serve with grace and charity.

"Let's have a catch!" That was, after all, what I was doing— having a catch. It never occurred to me then to wonder whether my brother or my friends were dreaming similar dreams to my own as they tossed a baseball from one side of the creosote-smelling August street to the other. Did they, as I did, in the moment they held the ball and fingered its red-stitched seams, see themselves dancing off third base, preparing to steal home to Jackie Robinson's rhythms? Did they see fantasy crowds as thick as fields of ripe wheat watching their every move? Did they transform reality into this almost unbearable passion for a boy's game? Was this how they, too, chose to view an adolescent's dream of fulfillment?

Curiously enough, I have never asked my brother these questions. Nor did I, forty years back, ask them of those friends who helped feed my fantasies of wholeness by tossing a baseball with me back and forth across the street. But I can still call up the blessings having a catch offered. There are rituals by which we feed the motions of the spirit. And I remember day after summer day leaning against a parked car, clawlike first baseman's mitt on my left hand, right crutch propped like a door jamb between shoulder and street so that I could maintain my balance. I watch the ball thrown from the other side of the street and wait until the very last moment before I snatch at it the way the graceful first baseman on the Yankees, George McQuinn, used to snatch balls from the air. And all the time, an imaginary play-by-play reverberates in my head, keyed to the sharp smack of the baseball hitting leather.

The experience of so intense an imaginary life can easily be codified, fitted to Erickson's idea of the seven stages of man or to any number of other theories of psychological compensation or to Freud's insistence on the dominance of Eros or Becker's insistence on the stronger dominance of death. I am content to note that among the gifts imagination bestows is the ability to avoid a too-early confrontation with one's true prospects. For me, throwing that baseball from one side of the street to the other was sufficient in itself. My fantasized talents were real enough in my mind to stave off the debts I would, sooner or later, be forced to recognize.

That was the way I played baseball, propped like a carefully balanced rock against a parked car as thousands cheered in my mind. And I loved the game even more than I had loved it before I was struck by polio. But as I look back, I loved even more the grace period it allowed me for the gradual acceptance of the idea that the physical life I had lost had been lost forever. In a curious way, a game I would engage in a passionate romance with for my entire life was most real to me, most vividly alive, as the fantasies it generated helped keep an untenable reality at bay.

Of all sports, baseball is most resistant to time. One worships its simple lines in some part of the mind at war with the very idea of time. Or perhaps it simply tempers our sense of time's passing by affirming the way we once were. These thoughts were themselves generated by an obituary I read while I ate my breakfast a few days ago. Roger "Doc" Cramer, who played in the major leagues for twenty years and who had 2705 hits to his credit, died over the weekend at the age of eighty-five. I suppose Doc Cramer was not a truly "great" player, but he could do everything a ballplayer was expected to do—hit, field, run, bunt, move a runner over—with style and grace. Throughout a long major league career, he was what used to be called a "ballplayer's ballplayer." Better still, Doc Cramer's name was on that baseball I held so worshipfully in my hands fifty years ago.

I have long since put an end to all hero worship. At least, I think I have. But if I close my eyes, I still see that ball, the signatures running into each other until I imagine a circle of names, with no beginning and no end, promising to bring me back to that time of my trial and the beginnings of my imagination's fulfillment. I think of how that ball helped me stave off recognitions that had to be held off until I was ready for them. And I find myself wishing that I could just say "Thank you" to Doc Cramer and to Hank Greenberg and to Skeeter Webb and to Rudy York and to Stubby Overmire (who, for some unexplainable reason, I have decided was the mysterious bullpen pitcher who pledged that baseball to my uncle) and to all those other dead players who kissed my need when I was a boy living in a hospital ward.

No doubt, a sentimental wish, not tough enough for an America in which baseball cards that no longer smell of bubble gum are sold for sums that would pay a present-day utility infielder's salary for an entire week. I am not really a man for so headily entrepreneurial a time. And I shouldn't have been surprised when I recently told the story of my autographed baseball to a colleague twenty years my junior and, voice tinged by excitement, he blurted out, "My God, do you know what that ball would be worth if you had it today?" And then, "What did you do with it?"

How do I tell him that what I did with it was to feed my illusions one last necessary time? For that was the ultimate gift that autographed baseball, talisman of my difficult years, offered me. For one final moment it helped me again hear the cheering in my head when I needed that cheering. Without my asking for it, the day would soon arrive when I would have no choice but to accept the prospects before me and recognize that I had better build a life as best I could because I was never going to play ball again. That autographed baseball was a casualty of my need for illusion. It missed its time of marketability because it had to be sacrificed to its owner's need for dreams.

One sunny weekday afternoon, I leaned against a parked car, propped in my ready-to-play position as my friend, Frankie, threw a baseball from one side of the street to the other. I had been having a difficult time in the field all afternoon, just as any major leaguer has days when he should have stayed in bed. The ball we were playing with had long since lost its cover, and it had been taped and retaped with that cheap, sticky black bandaging that New York City electricians were said to swear by.

Once again Frankie threw and once again I snatched at the ball, the tens of thousands of fans cluttering my mind beginning to get on me with catcalls and boos. But this turned out to be one snatch too many. The ball didn't fall to the ground this time. It simply hit my glove and, tape sticking to the mitt's webbing, unraveled, to collapse in a mass of dust and string before my brace-bound feet. Frankie rushed across the street and stared at the disintegrated dusty mass. He reached down, distastefully touching it as he might have touched a dead pigeon.

"That's it," Frankie said. "No more ball."

"I have a ball upstairs," I said, pulling a key from my pants pocket. "In the closet next to my bed."

Frankie went upstairs to my apartment and found the ball. He had seen it before, but he said nothing about the names etched across its yellowing leather skin. He knew, of course, who those heroes were. But we were having a catch and his priorities, like mine, were not yet glued to what modern-day Americans now view as a proper acquisition of investment capital. Besides, Frankie and I were American innocents in a nation whose sportswriters would never tag Doc Cramer with a name like "Charley Hustle." A signature was still just a name back then, and no one would have ventured to guess what its worth might ultimately be.

Still, there is a kind of justice even to memories of failed investments. Once we began to play with that autographed ball, I felt a renewed surety in my skill with a glove. I just couldn't miss what Frankie threw—as long, that is, as I could reach it. Unfortunately, even as the tens of thousands of onlookers in my head cheered my remarkable turnaround, my friend Frankie experienced a spell of wildness that made it easier for him to hit the brick wall of the apartment building behind me or the curbstone to my left and right than to hit my unerring mitt. One by one, the names on the ball disappeared, chalked and cut and scuffed into oblivion by granite and brick and creosote. That baseball autographed by the entire Detroit Tigers team on the day they clinched the pennant in 1945 would never again feed my illusions. For one last time, it had rescued me from a bad day. And those cheering fans, who rose as if one in my head to offer me the kind of ovation Stan "the Man" Musial would receive in Ebbetts Field after he had beaten my beloved Dodgers into submission, were voicing their approval of how that autographed baseball, that icon promising health in illness, had for this one last time snatched victory from potential disaster. There are, it turns out, different kinds of futures markets. And all sorts of marketability. In the final analysis, the bargain was mine—both to make and to keep.

7

HITTING
THE CLOCK

THE SCENE haunts me at the most unpredictable of times, a
seduction of both memory and desire. I can be sitting in a restaurant, across from my wife, talking into the life we have shared
over all these years, and, quite suddenly, I am there, thrust into
a single moment that somehow measures my life. A Saturday
morning in May, 1943, one week before I am to turn ten years
old. The immense pleasure, the renewed sense of expectation,
the emotional frame of a point in time—these have nothing to
do with my impending birthday. The body is my focus here, my
body. I watch that body crouch above an oblong piece of cardboard taken from somebody's father's laundered shirt and held
to the ground by a large gray stone. About to hit a baseball over
the ditch of the empty lot behind the block-long apartment
house known as Niles Gardens, I am still ignorant of all those
ironies that allow me to think of a name that rubs down to the
polished brass of English hunting horns as home. The name is
not foreign. For me, this America is knowledge enough. And the
language of this America is the English of street and alley and
city park.

A war is raging in the Europe my parents fled many years ago. In 1943, I think of that Europe not as a place but as a pungent Yiddish curse, a scorched earth of spit and imprecation. Magic and terror combined. *Ah srafah en deynah poonim.* A fire in your face. My parents endow the terror Europe evokes with a language I will eventually come to love but that still shames me in 1943. Neither Europe nor the Yiddish in which it is evoked is mine. And they will never be mine, not altogether. But this is 1943, and in the Bronx in which I live that Europe and that language still gauge reality, a measure of how far my parents have come. For me, Europe is somewhere in the distance, out there, beyond the beyond, beyond the gray vastness of the Atlantic— *der haym* to my mother and father, but just another spot on the map to me.

In any case, this pebble-strewn lot which we boys call the Backyard Field is a more meaningful piece of land than the Europe my parents have run from. In memory, each pebble tells me that I cannot choose the images that forever will lie in wait to ambush my ambition. Those images have already chosen me. Even in an overpriced French restaurant in Manhattan, talking to the woman I have loved for more years than I expected to live when we were married in 1957, places still anchor my sense of time. The Backyard Field stands between Niles Gardens and the small stores fronting Bainbridge Avenue, where my mother makes her daily shopping rounds. And here I crouch above the cardboard home plate, watching the pitch approach in a drift of agony and anticipation, red stitches clearly visible against the gray wartime substitute for leather that binds the ball to that brutal yet rich year of 1943.

Stuart Yahm is pitching. Thirty-three years later, at a party that is called to celebrate a book I have written about the neighborhood (no one at the party has read the book, and the party it-

self takes place not in the old neighborhood but in a Chinese restaurant on East 34th Street in Manhattan), I am to meet Stuart
Yahm again. At the party, we will talk about old times and, before he leaves to catch the red-eye to Los Angeles, he will hand
me a card that tells me he is a producer of rock-and-roll records.
Then we will laugh and embrace, like the strangers we have become, embarrassed at time's passing.

Only I am frozen with Stuart Yahm in 1943, just as I am frozen
into this single swing of a bat. As if in a slow-motion newsreel,
I watch my follow-through twist me into the child-muscled
grace of a still-unmarked not yet ten-year-old body. Once again,
I feel the rush of pleasure that tells me that my bat has met the
ball. I have hit it well. My left knee kisses the ground in exaggerated triumph as the ball sails out of the lot and high over
the rooftops linking one store to another on Bainbridge Avenue
in a black sweep of tarpaper. As if it had been caught by God's
invisible hand, the ball suddenly seems to halt in midair, like
a gull floating on the wind. And then the ball drops like a
buzz-bomb onto the large black clock hanging above the liquor
store.

Another monument in memory to remind me that in 1943 I
live in the same America that boys in Keokuk and Savannah and
Boise live in. It is difficult to romanticize that America during
a time as thick with accusation and reprimand and as short on
historical memory as our time has become. Call it racist, sexist,
homophobic, grudging, unforgiving—no doubt, the America of
1943 was all of these. Yet I still relish its clear boundaries, even
as, anchored above the liquor store, that black clock tells me
that the America in my mind is more real than any mere country
can possibly be.

The image of that America shelters me from the drab reality of this one, lingering in memory with a luminous glow and never wholly absorbed in time as it pushes me into the alternative future I will forever hunger for. In a world divided between "good guys" and "bad guys," America in 1943 is still "on God's side." That is what the heavyweight champ, Joe Louis, tells the nation on the night my Uncle Moe takes me to a war bond rally at Yankee Stadium. We are on God's side—Joe Louis, me, Stuart Yahm, Uncle Moe, all of us.

In 1943, American virtue seems as fixed as the evenly spaced trees lining the center of Mosholu Parkway. Those trees, which we boys use as first-down markers in October football scrimmages, will outlast even my Bronx provincialism, growing bigger year by year until they are killed off by an outbreak of Dutch Elm disease in 1969, when I am living in the Hague with my wife and two young sons. By then, both the liquor store and the clock will be long gone. Only in memory does that clock still loom above the liquor store, time's warden gazing down on the bored suburbanites lining up for the bus to Yonkers. Does that clock tell them, as it tells me, where we are—on this day, in this space, in that America?

Hitting the clock on the fly is like hitting the sign at Ebbets Field advertising a men's haberdashery store. For three years, Red Barber has fed my insatiable American lusts with his Southern accent and literate charm. At ten, I have no idea of what "a catbird seat" is, but when Red's mellifluous voice tells me we are sitting in one, I willingly suspend even the semblance of disbelief. Any player who hits a ball off the sign wins a suit of clothes from "Brooklyn's own, Abe Stark." In 1943, the prospect of so pedestrian a reward fails to stir the witch's brew of envy and ambition in my heart. Sartorial splendor is not what I want for hitting a baseball. What I want is beyond the giving power of any Brooklyn haberdashery king. I want the unending promise of this moment, the feel of my body, coiled like a taut spring, about to leap into a future as intimate as it is to be perfect.

I still want it.

Ten in the morning is too early for people living in my old neighborhood to buy liquor. It was the kind of neighborhood journalists and sociologists today like to speak of as "ethnically mixed"—Jews, Italians, Irish, the occasional "American" who must have looked on us not as strangers but as emblems of the new. And in this neighborhood, awaiting his afternoon trade, the owner of the liquor store sits in front of his glass window filled with bottles. He sits on a wooden milk crate, the seat of choice for anyone taking the sun in the Bronx of 1943. As if his body has been pasted together in doughy rolls of flesh, he looks like one of the wax figures of Vikings my classmates and I make in our social studies project at P.S. 80 on Rochambeau Avenue. Yet unlike those my fourth grade teacher calls "your Viking ancestors," the liquor store owner is alive, he is breathing, and he hears the ball strike his black clock. Without shifting his large bulk on the milk crate, he catches the ball before it can bounce into Bainbridge Avenue, where buses maneuver north and south like knowledgeable beetles. Or so Mr. Crimmi, the barber whose shop is next to the liquor store, tells me when he gives me my first ten-year-old haircut a week later. But I do not know this when I come running down Bainbridge Avenue and the fat liquor store owner grabs my shoulders and spins me around.

At first, I am afraid that the fat man is going to slap me or, worse still, lecture me about why I am not supposed to hit baseballs against his black clock. Clocks cost money. And money means trouble. My father has already had to pay Mr. Bregman, owner-superintendent of Niles Gardens, for a window I broke a week ago when I fouled a ball off into the Levy's living room. For my father, baseball is a threat. *Amerikanah chayah!* he yells at me. My father yells at me in Yiddish. He calls me an American animal. My father is right.

I love my father. But I am also secretly ashamed of him. My father is not an American father. Thirteen years in this country and he is still what is known as "a hard-working working man" in neighborhoods like ours. My father is grateful to this country and my father dreams American dreams. Only my father is not a success. And he is not destined to become a success. In his immigrant heart, my father imagines a future where he will someday be his own boss. On the day after I turn ten, he confides in me that he intends to buy the appetizing store two doors down from the liquor store. Mr. Wohl, the owner, is asking a mere five hundred dollars—for everything, stock, fixtures, and what he calls "good will." My father smiles as he tells me this. My father contemplates being an owner in America. My father is happy.

In the real future, my father is not destined to become an owner in America. My father will not be able to borrow the five hundred dollars from my Uncle Moe or from any of his other relatives. My father will remain much too cautious, much too European, unlike the fat man on the milk crate who grabs my shoulders. The man on the milk crate has an even thicker Yiddish accent than my father does, but he is already as American as I am. He does not yell at me in Yiddish. He does not lecture me on how sacred big black clocks are or angrily scold me as he tells me exactly how much they cost. Instead, he slaps me on the back, feeding the desire for triumph in his heart as well as my own. "Another Babe!" his spiced breath laughs, hooking a golden future to the raw splendor of my imagination. "Nuddah Bepp!" is how it actually comes out. Yet whatever the sound, music in memory remains music.

/ / /

Ultimately, my sense of aspiration will be overwhelmed by what the real future holds in store for me. Not that I am destined to become one of those men who curse fate and leave it at that. I may curse it on occasion, but I pride myself on how faithful I have remained to its demands. Please spare me any of those insufferable lectures about "living in the real world." I have made my way fairly well in that world for some time now. Long before I read Rousseau, I knew that I was as blank a slate as even his philosophically self-serving overblown ego might desire in a man. Only where most boys must wait until adolescence before being cast adrift, I was forced into what adults call "maturity" fourteen months after that morning I hit the clock on the fly.

To this day, I still tell myself that if polio hadn't struck me down I would have been the best ballplayer who ever emerged from the Bronx, better than big Hank Greenberg or the Fordham Flash, Frankie Frisch. Of course, I know that such thoughts are merely fantasies. And I never really believed the loose stuff of such fantasies. But I have always believed that memory is the true mother of justice. That being the case, what choice do I have but to hunger after my own unlived future? Never mind that the pride I take in my prowess masks the complexity of what disease has done to me. I know that the measure of a man's prowess remains in the eye of the beholder. So why expect me to settle for some drab reality when I can still hear the echo of that liquor store owner's, "Another Babe!" Pronunciation be damned! It's the promise of his words that I choose to believe. And that promise is testimony enough.

Why, when that boy is now a man of sixty, does he still linger over the pleasure of that swing like an adolescent lingering over the memory of his first kiss? Why do I still feel this rush of pleasure in wrists that tingle with the electric vibrations of bat meeting ball more than fifty years ago? Maybe the explanation is as simple as the image. For why do we expect sixty-year-old men to surrender the remnants of desire? Like prowess, logic, too, is in the eye of the beholder. Even a body thrust into its inexorable decline discovers that the dreams continue to stab at it with all the unforgiving need time magnifies. To match a talent as pedestrian as hitting a baseball with a moment frozen in memory offers a man a glimpse into the future that never was.

It's simply too easy to dismiss such fantasies as "childish." God knows, my dream is not that I want to play baseball again. I don't. The unlived future makes demands that are intense, but that doesn't mean they have to be banal. To a man of sixty, even baseball begins to grow boring. Age offers few gifts more welcome than distance from the self's most intense passions. It is one of the few aspects of growing older that one can wholeheartedly accept. Nonetheless, no other moment sticks to the ribs as tenaciously as that single swing of a bat that sent an ersatz baseball against a liquor store clock a half century ago.

In my late twenties, five years a husband and a recent father, I would fight the temptation of remembering the time I hit the clock the way an ex-smoker fights the desire to light up. Suddenly, unexpectedly, the image would steal upon me. And like the English teacher I had become, I would force memory into the subtlest of textual explications. Hitting the clock embodied a nostalgia so perverse that it threatened to wreak havoc on any chance I had to live a normal life. And when I was in my twenties, the desire to live a "normal life" was evidence of a mature and healthy outlook. I still believe that those of us forced to live with the leftovers of a serious illness should strive to live as "normally" as possible. But I have learned that my fascination with a future that fate did not allow me to live is as normal as today's emotionally overloaded America will permit.

One discovers differing ideas of what we call normalcy in this nation. It is fortunate for us that at least some of those ideas of normalcy seem safely beyond the tedious visions of blubbering campfire camaraderie that the gurus of the New American Masculinity insist we deserve. It seems to me far better to hit the black clock in memory than to seek the porous tear-stained cheeks of substitute Jungian fathers. I prefer one more imagined shot at the future that never was to the awful verbal ooze of psychobabble and victimization American men are now told they must bless in the name of love.

Nor am I, happily, the only man in America who feels this way. At a cocktail party I happened to attend a few years ago, I overheard a surgeon speak of the pleasure he felt at the age of fifteen, when he ran the table in his local poolroom. Repairing flesh and muscle and bone is how he now earns his living. Yet the talent he so terribly wanted to celebrate was not the talent that had brought him money and reputation. It is not his skill with a scalpel but running the table that speaks both for and to his remembered appetites. And that is understandable. For running the table offers him a different measure of who he was and what he once dreamed of becoming.

It is his own imagination whose pardon a man must ultimately learn to seek. That is why I understand why the businessman in his late forties who is sitting with a friend at the next table in the midtown restaurant where I am having dinner with my wife is reliving a college poker game. It is not vanity but that moment of fulfillment that feeds a man the sense of self he cannot do without. Once again, he asks for a single card. Only this time he knows that he will draw his inside straight flush. Whether prompted by fate or need, pulling that inside straight flush is memory's script. It is his moment, when the future was still unknown and when time still possessed all those possibilities he now can only look back on with envy. In his gambler's heart, that remains the moment framed by hope, the moment that will carry him into the future.

Such moments stand behind a man's sense that certain events in his life, however minor they may seem, are pivotal. Not that they can be changed or that the alternative future is to be had simply for the remembering. I do not seek my pre-crippled childhood in that recurrent image of hitting the clock. Nor am I at all oblivious to the painful truth that the future I search for lies in what is already the past. Yet even as I settle into my sixties, I still find myself subject to the pull of my unfulfilled ambitions—separated now from hope, framed against a physical decline whose inevitability is no longer theoretical.

What thrusts me into that time I hit the clock is what presses that surgeon to the time he ran the table or leads that businessman back to his inside straight flush. Memory holds not merely the events of our lives but all the desires and ambitions we once embraced—desires and ambitions each of us knows will never be fulfilled but which remain as painfully and gloriously intimate as they remain kinetically real.

Proust understood this well enough to create what is perhaps the greatest of all novels from the debris it left in his mind. But who is as courageous or as talented as our brave Gallic hypochondriac? Nor did Proust write his great novel while sitting around a campfire and weeping copious tears in some imitation prepubescent senility. He wrote it alone, in that famous cork-lined room, where he could return in memory and desire to those moments whose appeal even a great writer never fully comprehends. And he wrote it by recasting time itself to that terribly real if imprecise point before the choices were made and the imagined alternatives had not yet been cut short by "truth."

What is it I myself search for as I stride into that pitch and swing that bat again? Nothing so mundane as how well I could hit a baseball before my virus took me down. No, what I search for are all the possibilities that once resided in a future that did not yet reside in me. Despite that splendid description of Cleopatra floating down the Nile that Shakespeare puts into the mouth of Enobarbus, the truth is that age does, indeed, wither and custom does stale. And age does it to all of us, not just to that legendary Egyptian queen.

Yet even if death itself is lurking around the corner, it is memory and imagination, those two tempestuous lovers, who continue to speak to the moments in our lives before we were forced into the actual future. That is why, over and over again, that image of a boy crouching above a piece of cardboard pressed to earth by a stone returns to memory. It's not his lost prowess that boy is searching for, nor is it for legs still able to do what legs are supposed to do. It's for that single moment that may still be persuaded to carry him into his other past, to bring him home to that life he never lived and let him rest, if only for a brief interlude, in the alternative reality he still hungers for, where the real future waits to be claimed and where all a boy needs to make it his own is the courage to swing and to follow through.

8

SUPERMARKET MODERN

HOWEVER CURIOUS a passion for supermarkets may seem to others, it springs, like so much else in my life, from my childhood faith in egalitarianism. I love supermarkets both for what they are and for what they are not. I love them because they are among the places a man in America can unwind. I realize that men of my generation were conditioned to think of supermarkets as the province of women. And that may account for why masculinity can relax in a supermarket. Indeed, one of the glories of modern supermarkets, and one of the reasons one loves them, is that they tend to be neutral territory. I have yet to hear anyone, man or woman or child, pull rank or brag about family antecedents in a supermarket. Admittedly, I sometimes encounter rudeness in supermarkets. But rudeness is no more than an affirmation of the egalitarian temperament. In gym and poolroom, classroom and playing field, it is possible to establish a high stakes reputation. But the stakes in a supermarket are never higher for one individual than for the next. In supermarkets, reality alone is unbending. It's eat or die—for one and all.

My egalitarian fervor has been somewhat tempered as I've

grown older, but I still enjoy the loose, gregarious equality shopping in a supermarket offers. It may be that this speaks of nothing greater than the grudging accommodations each of us is forced to offer upon the altar of aging. Growing older teaches us to accept comfort wherever it is available. Youth may be served in bedroom, barroom, and board room, but so far as I can see it is of no particular advantage in a supermarket.

Whatever the source of my passion, I have always loved markets—of all kinds. As a child, before supermarkets became as familiar a sight in New York City as in Oshkosh, I would wander in and out of one small market after another. Clustered beehivelike alongside one another where Jerome Avenue hooked into Mosholu Parkway, those markets spoke of the rich, plebeian optimism that stained life in the North Central Bronx throughout the 1940s and 1950s. I was usually not very interested in what was being sold. Rather, my attention was commanded by the thrust and parry of buyer and seller as they went at each other. I loved those voices bargaining in English, Yiddish, and Italian while the Jerome Avenue El exploded overhead, adding its rattling chaos to our cacophony of commerce.

I am not always constant as a lover. At times, the appeal of markets lay dormant. And writers sometimes need less prosaic sources of inspiration than a market can provide. At eighteen, when I decided I was going to become a writer, I was as self-consciously "tough" as any of my peers. I preferred bars, jazz clubs, and East Village parties in old, decaying tenements to visits to Gristede's or the A&P. At eighteen, I toed manhood's line in emulation of Hemingway, cultivating the display of appetite more than appetite itself. Like all callow and inexperienced young men, I assumed the stance of someone who wanted to be viewed as hard and weathered. And whatever attractions supermarkets possess, they were never meant to appeal to a young man's burgeoning sense of manhood.

But as I grew older, I began to store part of my sense of a writer's reality in a corner of America usually removed from the concerns of literature. It was not, I suppose, totally unexpected. Turn a writer's debts to the public eye and, if nothing else, you will understand where he stakes his allegiances. His taste may strike the reader as peculiar or even pedestrian, but that does not mean it is not a taste that has been earned. In my case, this meant that I looked at supermarkets as a true believer views church or synagogue or mosque—rightly or wrongly, their existence is curiously reassuring.

Yet when I entered a supermarket, it was with specific expectations. Even in an age as wild about celebrity as ours is, I would never anticipate meeting an Elizabeth Taylor or a Michael Jordan in the aisles of my neighborhood D'Agostino on Twenty-Third Street. If I want to see celebrities in their glorified flesh, I simply travel three blocks north to Madison Square Garden or else drive crosstown to some East Side bistro that the rich and famous are rumored to frequent. After all, celebrities must be visible in order to remain celebrities. Part of the job of being known is that one must watch other celebrities as they, too, do their thing. Before he announced to the world that he was HIV positive, Magic Johnson would find himself cheered at courtside by Jack Nicholson, invariably described as "that passionate Lakers' fan, Jack Nicholson, the famous actor." It was understood by one and all that Jack was both a passionate Lakers' fan as well as a famous actor. Nonetheless, I suspect that he was also carrying out the obligation one celebrity feels to watch another celebrity strut his stuff. Imagination balks at the image of Jack jumping up and down on the sidelines as he roots for Magic to backhand a ripe cantaloupe or palm the juiciest sirloin.

I suspect that George Bush's defeat in the election of 1992 had something to do with his venturing into a supermarket, trying to pretend that he was "just folks." Bush was probably smart enough to understand that God did not intend for him to venture into supermarkets. Men know where they feel uncomfortable and out of place. Yet if George Bush was a child of privilege, he was also a lifelong politician, which meant that he had been told, over and over again, to pretend to be "just one of the boys." One can envision certain politicians hefting grapefruits or pausing at the dairy shelves to mull over the price of a wedge of cheddar. But George Herbert Walker Bush in a supermarket was one more election-year prop, as politically subliminal as the flag or Willie Horton. Ordinary men search for the weekly specials in a supermarket. George Bush just wanted a photo opportunity session. It's no wonder that he lost.

Merely in creating the possibility of a good hot shower, Edmund Wilson once wrote, indoor plumbing has proven of greater benefit to mankind than the Cathedral of Chartres. I suspect Mr. Wilson was correct in this, as he was correct in so much else. And as my immigrant grandmother was always quick to remind me, "Who are you to argue with such a great man?" Nonetheless, permit me to voice one nervous cavil to the great man's dictum: When it comes to making the creative juices flow, a brightly lit supermarket is even better than indoor plumbing.

This is particularly true for men in supermarkets. For if a man's sense of reality is in danger of running down, few places recharge it better than a modern supermarket—which is why I used to do the shopping for the family, a fact my wife and two sons still view with a certain incredulity. Sooner or later, they were afraid, I was going to demand that they share in "the burdens of shopping." What they couldn't understand was that those very burdens told me that my world still turns on its axis, and that, whether or not God was in his heaven, there were certain moments when all was, indeed, right with the world.

/ / /

Aging has not only allowed me to admit that supermarkets fascinate me, it has also allowed me to acknowledge that I am far more my father's son than I once believed possible. In my old neighborhood, one of the things all children knew was that ethnic groups could be identified by what the men in the family did for a living. Most Jews worked in the fur and garment industries; while most Italians worked in construction or in fruits and vegetables. The Irish, our subaltern WASPs, worked "for the city." My father was a counterman in an appetizing store.

All three of my uncles were furriers, so my father's line of work evoked a certain amount of comment in our family. While he bitterly referred to himself as "a horse," and while he worked much longer hours for considerably less pay than my uncles did, my father did not, to my knowledge, regret his choice of a vocation. He sliced smoked salmon and pickled herring, rolled huge wooden vats of pickles soaked in brine onto the Jerome Avenue sidewalk early each morning, and turned himself into an authority on an exotic miscellany of foods—rock candy and cottage cheese, halvah and lake sturgeon, kippered salmon and pickled peppers.

Food was something my father understood intimately. In the Polish shtetl from which he had emigrated, his father, my grandfather, had owned and worked a small mill. Food stained my father's life—not merely the profusion of it but the ceremonies associated with it. Just as the synagogue was as much a repository of memory as of worship, so to see a market brimming with food filled my father with a sense of God's abundance.

He was "an appetizing man"—as vain about working the counter rather than stocking shelves as the full professor is vain about teaching a graduate seminar in Chaucer rather than teaching freshman comp. Most men take their vanity where they find it. My father took his wherever he could. No sentimental Chagall canvas would float his shtetl soul for the world's view. In his eyes, as in the eyes of most other men in the neighborhood, a man was what a man did. Even here in America, *der goldenah medinah*, a man's work was what defined him.

More of that sensibility has rubbed off on me than I care to admit. Among the many enticements I find in the modern supermarket is the sweep of color that confronts me as soon as I walk past its electronic eye portals. And chief among the reasons why the appetizing and deli department—the kind of market within a market my father worked in until the day he died—appeals to me so much is that here plastic does not usually come between the customer and the smell of food. In my father's time, orders were handed to the customer wrapped in wax paper or oil paper. To an appetizing man—and to an appetizing man's son—the smell of food is as important as its taste.

When I first took sick with polio, my father was called from the market where he worked and sent, along with my terrified mother, to the small hospital some seventy miles north of New York where I lay board stiff even as the virus charged up from my toes as relentlessly as Babel's Cossack Cavalry. My father had been telephoned at work from the hospital, and he and my mother had then been driven down to Grand Central Station by his boss. He had not had time to change his clothes or to bathe, and he sat alongside my bed in the small hospital in Cold Spring, imploring me to live and feeding me vanilla ice cream. What remains as vivid in memory today as it was more than fifty years ago is the odor that clung to my father's hand as he fed me that ice cream. I could smell the dry-sweat prospect of my death on that hand. Yet beyond that, overwhelming death, was the smell of pickle brine and smoked salmon and chopped herring that mixed with the rich creamy taste of the vanilla ice cream. For whatever incomprehensible reason, the mixing of smells was a father's promise to a son that he would live.

I can't say it any more clearly than that. Nothing, absolutely nothing—not a hot dog at Yankee Stadium, not the first fish I caught which my wife then cooked crusted with bread crumbs and lime, not a memorable meal at Le Pre Catalan in 1985's ten-francs-to-the-dollar Paris—ever smelled that good again. The smells that feed one hope are not necessarily decorous and they are, God knows, difficult to replicate—even in a writer's imagination. But I remember the smell of his hand as the smell of the market, that wonderful mix of food and life. In some corner of my mind, the smell lingering on that hand still links itself to life and to that blessed moment when my resistance to death began. It is a smell that structures memory, a smell as sharp and thin as a razor's stroke, forever frozen to hope and to the resurrection not of the soul but of the body.

Whenever I travel, I try to take the temperature of the local citizenry. There are any number of ways one can do this—randomly wandering through the nearest park, nursing a beer in a local bar, surveying newspapers and magazines at the corner drugstore or WalMart checkout counter. But there is nothing I enjoy more than a visit to the supermarket. And not merely because it tells me more about the local populace than I will discover in bar or park or WalMart, but because it seems to establish a certain neighborhood tone, one that often reveals more than I can find out elsewhere.

Shopping demands definition through style. And supermarket shopping demands as much style as haute couture shopping on the rue Rivoli. For one thing, neither women nor men think it is important to be on their best behavior in supermarkets. They do not guard the inner person, fearful of being exposed. No matter how frequently people shop in supermarkets, they probe the atmosphere in the same way that they probe the merchandise. But it is their own selves they are really probing, even as they move from aisle to aisle, projecting their ease with the neighborhood and the neighborhood's ease with itself.

In April 1965 my wife and I and our two-year-old son spent a month in Paris. We had come there from the Netherlands, where we had been living since September. Ted Gross, a friend and colleague who was also on a Fulbright that year, had generously offered us the use of his apartment in Paris while he and his family were on vacation. The apartment was in the Eighth Arrondissement, on the rue Passy, tucked inside an attractive cobblestone courtyard stamped by that essential turn-of-the century architecture that marks Paris with such surety. One emerged from that courtyard into a family bakery that filled the street with its rich fresh smells. Each morning, Harriet would go downstairs and buy our breakfast croissants there.

Across the street from the bakery, hooked around a small bar where, remembering Hemingway, I made it a point to drink, a bit too self-consciously, I confess, a brandy each afternoon, stood the entrance to what was one of the first supermarkets in Paris. In 1965, De Gaulle was urging the French to smile at all foreigners, particularly Americans. While we Americans might be lacking in *la gloire*, we were still laden with dollars at a time when the dollar connoted power in Europe. It was a time in which the virtues of the small shopkeeper were constantly being extolled as the bone and marrow of French civilization. In that Paris whose citizens were encouraged to smile at foreigners, Harriet stumbled upon our first European supermarket while pushing our two-year-old son's stroller through the streets of the Eighth Arrondissement. Armed with the desire to see what an American intrusion on Parisian grandeur might be, she pushed her way inside. What, she wondered, would shopping in INNO (the supermarket's name) be like.

It was remarkably similar, it turned out, to shopping in a New York A&P or Grand Union. In Noordwijk-Aan-Zee, there was nothing even remotely resembling an American supermarket in 1965. In Noordwijk, we strolled with our son every Wednesday afternoon through the outdoor market, buying cheese and hot syrup waffles and fried fish, conscious of how well we fit in. Yet as much as we enjoyed the quaintness of that old Europe, we both sensed that this weekly outdoor market was already an anachronism, doomed to go the way of the small markets of my childhood that had once burrowed up and down Jerome Avenue. We have not been back to Noordwijk since 1965, but both of us would be surprised if it does not by now contain a number of supermarkets.

For modern shopping reflects modern life—and just as a hot shower may have been more beneficial to human development than the building of Chartres Cathedral, so the supermarket offers not only abundance but the kind of comfort from which a man scans his own life's choices. If we have learned nothing else from the collapse of Marxism, we should at least acknowledge democracy as the one true leveler of the world. And a supermarket is nothing if not democratic. "Kings as clowns are codgers," wrote Melville, "who ain't a nobody?" It's a line I have always loved for its egalitarian regency, as well as its sense of limited possibility, a great writer's belief that while all roads lead to defeat, one's journey is nonetheless filled with the baubles of being human. Melville's line embraces the nature of the modern supermarket, even in bourgeois Paris.

No matter how large a supermarket may be, and I remember that INNO in Paris as huge, immense, it cannot exist without being part of its neighborhood. Supermarkets are specific, regional, grounded in the tastes and fears of local men and women.

Even if a company stretches, as the A&P's name brags, from ocean to ocean, the supermarket must remain particular to the locale in which it is set down. "Where shrimp boats dock," a shrimper told me on a cold January day a few winters ago, "shrimp rules the market." In South Carolina's Low Country, where I now spend my winters, supermarkets are expected to accentuate the local. And they are expected to feature local wares by all, not merely a shrimper accusing the Chinese of dumping shrimp the way the Japanese dump steel—beating our naive American brains out. As sure as God made apples, this shrimper knew that the shrimp in Food Lion or Winn-Dixie or Piggly-Wiggly were local. There are lines beyond which even those free-market forces so regularly invoked on CNN dare not journey.

A need for the regional was as much in evidence in the Paris of 1965 as in the South Carolina Low Country of 1992. The French had not yet given up on *la gloire* and had not yet accepted their diminished role in the world. In 1965, the eye they cast at the rest of Europe was skeptical and grudging. Not even those small Parisian shopkeepers—disgruntled Poujadistes and embittered ex-settlers returned from an Algeria they remembered with a fierce nostalgia of possession—could envision a free market that would ultimately re-make them thoroughly. The light shining on that football field of an INNO burst upon me with all the brilliance of a clear sunlit morning, while the family bakery in which Harriet purchased our breakfast croissants each morning was dim and sedate, husband and wife owners and two women clerks pinching pennies from an age-old frugality as engrafted on them as the rhetoric of *la gloire*. Were the shopping fields of INNO nothing more than an invitation to the conspiracies of betrayal? Even if they had been, should that have mattered? Guilt and confession were noticeably out-of-place in the modern supermarket.

/   /   /

Plebeian ambitions, a democracy of taste in which Sandra's palate is as easily satisfied as Steve's—that is what counts in supermarkets. Cry "Yes!" to the waves of food. Apples, pears, bananas, grapes, strawberries—food in boxes, food in bunches, food in mounds or piles or bulging against netting designed not to hold in but to show off all that is plump and juicy and beckoning. Red salamis wrapped in cellophane, cartons of orange juice arranged as if they were soldiers on parade, embankments of frozen food as precisely spaced as horse guards at attention in front of Buckingham Palace—a carnival in which price is overwhelmed by sight. Yellows, oranges, browns, reds, greens, a drunken rush of color spread against the market's canvas by some assistant manager let loose to cultivate the Picasso lurking in his soul. Lines of temptation that scatter east and west, north and south, beckoning and thrusting off and then primping with possession, as if Proust had invited Klee to accompany him to the Beaux Arts Ball. Linoleum square patterns of white and red, red and orange, green and gold, to hunt down the glint of passion in Mondrian's electric eye. Junkies of color drenched in the ease of their aspirations. From one end of America to the other, a Mardi Gras of plenitude lasting 365 days a year, strung out like lights on the Christmas tree in Rockefeller Center.

A good supermarket invites us to walk through its splendors like true practitioners of the art of selection. Here is the authentic American dream. When I was a schoolboy and stood with my fellows, adding my own voice to the swelling chorus of "America, the Beautiful" during Wednesday morning assemblies, I used to close my eyes when I came to the words, "fruited plain." Until the supermarket entered my consciousness, I simply could not envision America's fruited plains. I would think of a level green billiard table of a map topped by grapefruit and grape, pear and apple and orange, fish and fowl, cottage cheese and cream cheese and cheddar—like one's toppings of choice on an ice cream sundae. But once the supermarket arrived in ethnic New York—and swept into my line of vision, too, as it had already swept through the rest of this America—I understood what that fruited plain meant. Abundance without choice is meaningless. Along with the Met and MOMA, supermarkets taught me that.

I spent a recent winter down South, trying to begin a novel. Sometimes, the fictional world I was trying to create would press against me, threatening to blind me to the sight of beach and pelican below my window. As if a warning light had turned on in my head, I would quit my desk and drive to a supermarket that had become a particular favorite of mine, a Food Lion anchoring one of those ubiquitous shopping malls one finds throughout the nation. My novel was to be set in Germany during the early 1970s, and perhaps my way of acknowledging its pressures was to flee them for the firmer presence of those displays of fruits and vegetables boxed in by space and proportion. "Fruited plain" enough! In fiction, the landscape rolled to the beat of our century's raging turbulence of loss—my murdered uncles and aunts and cousins, the aftermath of the Holocaust for Jew and German, the postwar political terrorism of Baader-Meinhof. A wax museum of contemporary horrors. I suspect that I would retreat to supermarket abundance in order to feel the touch of human scale, that sense of proportion that displays of food allow us.

Writers have no choice but to believe in the landscapes they themselves create. Yet one sometimes needs to step back and breathe deeply. Even in giving voice to turbulence, one has to feel for the pulse of the ordinary. How better to do that than by enmeshing the self in the planet's abundance? In a supermarket, private life is public by default. There are no secrets here, no choices to bring one shame. Salsa or ketchup, chile hot or mild—

for black or white, Gentile or Jew, rich or poor, man or woman, in supermarkets the only meaningful questions are fresh or canned or frozen. Kinships are not of the blood but of taste alone.

I am shopping in a supermarket in Albuquerque in the summer of 1977, standing before row upon row of canned beans, embarrassed by my ignorance, trying to convince myself that choosing one brand over another is that and nothing more. "Choice is not destiny," I whisper aloud. I cannot even seek guidance from a lifelong childhood loyalty to Heinz and its fifty-seven varieties. Heinz Vegetarian Beans, which to my mother was an article of symbolic faith, rather like her own arrival in America in 1920 on George Washington's birthday—cannot be seen in the piled mountains of cans before me. The American West is not ethnic Pittsburgh or New York City. Even in 1977, supermarkets in the city of my birth are small, tighter than they are in the rest of America. In New York, space is at a premium. Out west, space is a given, as obvious as the mountains or the dry air.

A stranger taps me on the shoulder. I turn with the hard uncertain irritation of a man who is unable to make up his mind. The stranger's New Mexican face is swarthy, flattened into the long depths of his deep black eyes and black hair and dark subtly lined forehead. Indian, Hispanic, Anglo—the mixture doesn't matter. Not to him and not to me. Choice is American. He and I are in this supermarket together. He points to a bright yellow can with a picture of dark red pinto beans. "Those," he says, "are the best."

"Thanks," I say, taking two cans and dropping them into the shopping cart. I feel relieved. "There are so many." He nods again, moves toward frozen foods, and disappears, a Westerner at peace with the abundance of choice in America.

/ / /

A supermarket should not be a breeding ground for a man's discontent. It should not be the kind of place that is forced to placate the demands of a man's ego. Yet if untrammeled ego alone now defines us (Norman Mailer accurately terms ego our century's "great word"), then the supermarket will ultimately be as foreign to the thrust of our America as Jefferson's idea that the country undergo a new revolution every twenty years. Perhaps ego will not triumph. Mailer, I remind myself, has never been a writer to scratch around in the alleys of the common and pedestrian. The kind of working people he writes about are boxers, street urchins transformed into professors, Mafiosi quick to take offense at the hint of a snub. No mechanics or assembly line workers. No furriers or appetizing clerks. One meets his people not in supermarkets but in roadside 7-Elevens, "coffee and" or "coke and" already half devoured as they walk back to the car.

Not only do supermarkets offer a density and variety nowhere visible in the stripped-down functionalism of the 7-Eleven, they also demand allegiance to the range of choice and possibility America offers. They embody optimism. In spirit, they belong to the 1950s, when choice and responsibility melded in this country. They measure the nation's fears and aspirations—a more accurate gauge of how we became what we are than either Le Cirque or McDonald's. Not monumental fears and not monumental aspirations—but the rising everyday expectations that crackled from Florida to Maine, from California to Virginia. Supermarkets were never intended to make Americans acknowledge discontent. The future they trumpet is not orgiastic but solid, opulent. No one feels the need to be larger than life in a supermarket. For supermarkets do not suggest that ego will gnaw at one's insides like a tapeworm devouring the psyche.

In the Food Lion in South Carolina, I seek a touch of the human. Deli man, butcher, clerk stocking shelves, the assistant manager who fills in at the checkout counter at lunchtime—as they did in the Bronx of my childhood, here, too, a job provides definition. But here such definition is luck or fate, not character. The men and women who work in Food Lion are no different from the men and women they serve. If I ask about prices or where to find an item, they are ready with an answer. It is what they are paid to do.

I'm certain that they, too, have mornings when they wake ready to grind the world down to their rage—but not because they consider working in a supermarket demeaning. Not like in my New York. Other than its taxi drivers, nothing signifies the decline of this city better than the people who work in its super-markets. "I'm a horse," my father would say, defining himself even as he urged me to study, learn, master a profession. Maybe he was. But memory's vision is of a man who sliced smoked salmon and pickled herring, a yellow number two pencil behind his ear, ready to stab at the brown paper bag on which he added the prices with speed and accuracy.

Working in a supermarket, my father could maintain his pride and feed his family. Work was dignity, a difficult phrase to write for anyone who remembers the consequences cloaked by *Arbeit Macht Frei*. Nonetheless, the supermarket in the housing co-op in which I have lived for these past thirty-five years still stabi-lizes my sense of life in New York. Appetizing man, grocery clerk, woman behind the checkout counter—work, a job, a function.

Only now my co-op supermarket has been taken over by a chain, and the young men behind the appetizing counter stand defenseless before the reign of the computer, weights and mea-sures defined, printed, stamped into their fear. America was dif-ferent in the 1950s, where so much of my own memory still re-sides. Supermarkets, interstate highways, the glass boxes lining

Park Avenue—the promise of abundance was to be found in the triumph of the modern. Now, like those who are aging everywhere, I measure time through the ease it bestows on my own passage through. It is not memory that imprisons me but my growing impatience with suffering. In this New York, one is supposed to take suffering for granted—and suffering is not really visible in a supermarket.

I stand with my wife on the corner of Eighth Avenue and Twenty-Sixth Street. Harriet hails a cab. I hear her tell the driver she wants to go to Lincoln Center. The sullen shrug of his shoulders indicates that he does not know where Lincoln Center is. A half hour later, wondering whether Harriet got to the theater before curtain time, I stand before the young girl at the checkout counter of the supermarket. The tape in the register has run out. The girl searches for the assistant manager. She is literally terrified. *He* knows how to change the tape. At eighteen, she is a cashier in a supermarket and she is already obsolescent in this America. I think of my father. Immigrant, horse, appetizing man. In the midst of this supermarket abundance, I turn my face away, suddenly swept by rage and shame, here, in my America.

PART IV

RELATIONS

9

PURSUING WOMEN, MEETING MYSELF

Is there a better way to focus on the pursuit of women than to begin with that famous line of Freud's, "What is it that women want?" The line commands response, as an acknowledgment of exasperation by any important intellectual figure is bound to do. Among other things, it speaks of a frustration with women that may be closer to indifference than Freud himself could afford to believe. There is an innocence to Freud's exasperation that is striking. While men only sometimes pay for indifference, they almost always pay for innocence. Given how much heavy feminist artillery has been aimed at Freud for that single remark, we owe the good doctor a substantial debt for having taken a pounding for us all.

Like most men I know, I often find myself bewildered by women. I suspect that Freud at times felt equally bewildered. But whereas most men do not speak of their bewilderment, Freud gave voice to his. In the process, he deflected a good deal of feminist anger that might otherwise have been directed toward men-at-large. Other than that equally infamous prayer in which orthodox Jewish men thank a decisively male Jehovah for the "blessing" of not having been made women, few remarks have been more consistently or more savagely held up to scorn by feminists. And probably for good reason: Freud wanted his women too clear and too simple.

By now, we men should have learned enough about relations between the sexes to understand that the best we can hope for is to figure out what it is that we want from women. As Freud should have realized, that is going to be difficult for all of us. It certainly was difficult for me. Yet ever since a month before I turned seventeen, when I consciously set about to make myself more interesting and more attractive to women (or "girls," as even fifty-year-old men could still refer to women during that verbally innocent, unliberated year, 1950), I have consistently, selfishly, and vigorously focused on what it is I need and want from women. As so often proves the case, it turns out that what I need and want is a different view of myself.

At seventeen, the pursuit of women didn't set me apart from the vast majority of American males trying to uncover the mysteries through which adolescent boys became men. If anything, I had come to the pursuit late, having spent the years between eleven and sixteen—years during which most other boys I knew were closely focused on what they wanted from girls—alternating between a critical need of a fantasy life and what, in retrospect, seems a rather healthy determination to adapt to living the rest of my life with useless legs.

Of course, I understand now that through facing what it is they want from women, adolescent boys are just trying to fashion the terms they must live with as men. But I didn't know that at seventeen. I had only just begun to admit to the idea that whether I faced a woman as friend or lover, there were certain obligations I simply had to meet. As the butting head of reality rammed against my fantasy life and pounded it out of shape, I came to see that I had few choices where women were concerned. Necessity may or may not be the mother of invention, but it is certainly the aggressive father of a man's sense of reality. There was no way to avoid facing women the same way I had to face men—with the brace-bound legs and crutch-holding arms of a cripple. Although five and a half years had passed since polio claimed my legs, not until I was almost seventeen was I truly ready to admit that the results were permanent and unalterable. Cripple I was, cripple I would remain. It may not sound like much, but it was a major admission, a painful admission, for me to make. I couldn't make it until I was forced to admit to myself that I had no other choice. One learns to take a certain confidence as well as a certain desperation from reality—if the problems it poses are clearly defined.

Perhaps five and a half years sounds like more than enough time for me to have learned to adjust to my future. It probably was. But I am talking, remember, about the years of my adolescence. And what was true of normal adolescents was even truer of me. Adolescents are not particularly adept at handling loss of any kind. Not should they be expected to be. Exactly how can any adolescent, male or female, handle the loss of a part of the body? In my own case, the answer was to grab at every escape hatch imagination presented. For better or worse, I was an imaginative child. And so for almost six years, I had dealt with being crippled by avoiding its actual consequences. It was simply easier to dream time and reality away.

That was especially true when I found myself thinking— "daydreaming" is the more accurate word—about girls. I know that thinking about girls takes up a disproportionate amount of any male adolescent's time. Occasionally, I would find myself standing, speechless with embarrassment, on my braces and crutches in front of a girl on whom I had developed a crush, if that is what my vague dreams of sex can be called. She lived in an apartment two floors above ours. With an ease that seems remarkable at this point, I would retreat into the privacy of our apartment, there to construct a fantasy body sculpted in part by Hollywood and in part by some offspring of Praxiteles. Once I possessed that, nothing could come between me and that girl, or, for that matter, between me and whatever woman I had made into the object of desire—the gorgeous Elizabeth Taylor, say. There was, of course, the minor reality of flesh and bone and muscle. But in fantasies, such minor realities could be disposed of quite easily.

Not that I chose a fantasy life. It is more accurate to write that my fantasy life chose me. In fantasy, I simply discovered that I could be anything imagination demanded I be—cowboy or Indian, ballplayer or boxer, warrior or lover. Among the blessings of having too much time on one's hands—until the age of seventeen, I spent most of my time alone in a small apartment, even my schooling provided by a teacher who would instruct me in the kitchen for an hour three times weekly—was that I learned to try on roles the way normal adolescents tried on clothes. Like them, I was searching for the proper fit.

Not until then was my unconscious forced to take a great leap forward with the recognition that the loss of my legs was permanent. Before that, it was simply too difficult to give up the fantasy of waking up one morning to find that I was once again in possession of a normal body. The mind is a subtle owner, a grasping landlord even of its fantasies. It will obscure any reality that it finds too painful to accept—among them, that the pursuit of women probably should not even begin until a man can acknowledge the fears dominating his life. Yet one's mind also extracts a rather considerable price for allowing the fantasies to endure. In the final analysis, it was my mind that forced me to surrender the refuge of fantasy and to acknowledge the way things were.

Had Freud been a little less single-minded, and less closely focused on the dark subterranean flow of the unconscious, he might have been able to force us to acknowledge the reality principle far more readily than we seem willing to do. We are, each of us, victims of our own rhetorical recycling. Not even Freud was apparently capable of asking the question men really need answered, "What is it that we want from women?"

No one could be more intrigued by the self emerging from its cocoon than I was as a seventeen-year-old cripple. I was absolutely absorbed by my own image. But self-absorption isn't necessarily narcissistic. I simply began to study myself, to look closely at how I behaved with girls and how I appeared to them. I tried to be as objective as possible about this self I was just getting to call my own. Having just begun to realize that I needed to make myself over, I recognized that my problem was not merely my own physical survival; it was how to make my survival appealing to girls. I was so intensely attuned to the demands of disease that I approached the problem with a naiveté that would have been amazing in a normal seventeen-year-old male.

Poets work at making language new by making it vivid and dramatic: I approached the task of making the self new by making it vivid and dramatic with as much dedication as any fledgling poet. If I wanted women to like me, I thought, then I had to confront myself—both as I was, standing on those double long-legged braces with crutches thrust beneath my shoulders, and as I wanted to be, a man able to define both limitation and possibility for himself. How could I exploit the physical powers I had lost? Like Lermontov, I needed to create a hero for our time. Only in my case, the hero had to be me.

Vanity is the only sin that remains unchanged even after one confesses to it. It could be argued, in fact, that the sin grows in the confession. A strategic sin, vanity is a powerful motivator. If it is easy to stand on the sidelines—observing the behavior of others, categorizing, labeling, measuring, quantifying the self as one learns to quantify single-celled organisms in high school biology—it is not easy to deal with one's own creation myths. During my five and a half years of living as a cripple, I managed to avoid thinking about how girls responded to my presence—by which, of course, I mean the fact of my being crippled. If such a prospect threatened to open too many dangerous avenues, I was probably better off not knowing. Or so I told myself. I cannot remember, at any time during those years, ever asking myself what it was a girl actually saw when I stood before her. Nor can I remember ever thinking about whether or not girls reacted differently to my physical disability than men did.

I knew that I had been fortunate in that polio had taken my legs rather than my arms. However dependent I might have been upon my fantasies, by the time I was seventeen I had at least learned that there were few ways in which hands and arms couldn't be transformed into usable substitutes for legs. One could drive a car without legs; one could swim without legs (I first learned to swim while in the hospital); one could read books and one could listen to jazz and, best of all, one could dream dreams of conquest without legs. And in those dreams, one could even travel throughout the world without legs. Given those possibilities, I managed to avoid thinking about how one could make love without legs.

I remember sitting in a darkened movie theater one afternoon, shortly after the pull of fantasy had been broken. I was watching Marlon Brando in his first film, Stanley Kramer's *The Men*. Although I had spent eighteen months spinning in a wheelchair through the corridors of the state hospital in which I lived, Brando simply seemed more natural in his wheelchair than I had been in mine. Curiously, I felt jealous as I watched him push himself through a V.A. ward. Still, even at seventeen, I was able to joke about my jealousy of how adroitly Brando could handle a wheelchair. Looking back, what strikes me as a much more interesting reaction—one I neither joked about nor allowed myself to think about—was how I kept wondering how the paraplegic Brando was going to make love to the healthy, determined, thoroughly middle-class Teresa Wright. How, in short, was Brando's All-American para going to do it? How did a cripple fuck?

Of course, movies made in 1949, no matter how "realistic," didn't contain scenes of actual lovemaking. It was one thing to be realistic about men in wheelchairs (despite the Dr. Kildare movies of the 1940s, even that was considered daring in 1950), quite another to show them confronting paraplegic sex. *The Men* could be graphic about the wounds the vets in the ward suffered and the treatment they had to endure. Yet aside from a brief scene in which the physician speaks to a group of wives and girlfriends about a paraplegic's ability to make love, sex is not among the problems that the film tackles. I should note that *The Men* was a valiant film, if a bit too self-conscious. To his credit, Stanley Kramer tried to be honest about the pain of bodily loss. (In one memorable scene, just after they have been married Teresa Wright stares as Brando's legs spasm uncontrollably, while he sits, rage growing, in his wheelchair watching her watch him.) But the film couldn't teach me how a man with dead legs fucked.

Now, of course, I realize that I had no right to expect it to. I would have to learn that by myself, as men have learned to be lovers ever since Adam cast a widening eye at Eve's flesh, tempting him beneath its fig-leaf covering. *The Men* was trapped by the proprieties of its age. And I was trapped as well. For among the messages disease teaches a cripple, particularly if that cripple is an adolescent, is the need to be cautious. All failure is a potential killer when it involves the risks of the heart. For failure kills aspiring normal lovers, too. And rarely does it kill them painlessly. How could Stanley Kramer possibly have understood the price of failure for a cripple? If he had, he would have made a different movie, in which the paraplegic Brando pursues the unmaimed Teresa Wright like a hawk swooping down on its kill. Both paraplegic man and middle-class woman had a great deal of learning to do. In my own pursuit of women, it turned out that I had even more.

How often did I find myself wishing, when I was sixteen, that the therapists who had spent so much time in the hospital teaching me how to mount a wooden mock-up of the steps of a New York City bus or how to climb a flight of stairs on braces and crutches had also somehow found a way to teach me what I really needed to know—how a man without the use of his legs can be sexually arousing. How I wish they had taught me that love, too, is dependent upon the discipline of heart and mind and imagination. Such a lesson would not only have been deeply reassuring, it might have led me out into the nonfantasy world a lot earlier.

In the long run, a cripple learns how to mount a bus or walk up and down a staircase through trial and error. Experience really is the best teacher. But I was not looking for somebody else's sexual experience. I wasn't looking for the kind of textbook approach to sexuality that is peddled in airports and department stores in gruesomely matter-of-fact manuals of sexual technique, all of them guaranteeing to make one's sexual life "new." What I was looking for was far more profound—the reassurance that derives not from the prospect of pleasure but from the task of achieving an individual self. What is it that men want from women? No less a gift than being a singular man.

Sex and sexuality had already been turned into a "subject" in postwar America, like civics or hygiene. Through some curious osmosis, Americans had made themselves over into a people who talked incessantly about "relationships" and "the unconscious." (Has there ever been a decade in which more people sounded off about "the Oedipus complex" and "penis envy" than the ten years following World War II?) And the more people talked about sex, the less certainty they seemed to feel about it. If a normal adolescent didn't know what to do about sex, why should a seventeen-year-old cripple have known?

What is it that men want from women? Among other things, it seems to me that they want the sexual self one possesses to be the sexual self one creates. It is possible to dramatize anything—including the physical limitations that threaten to define every area of a man's life. Better than learning to drive or learning to swim or even learning what I never did manage to learn, how to fly, was learning that one could transform the self. A man could set about deconstructing his own psyche in order to reconstruct his body.

Like any venture capitalist risking substance by betting on his hunches, I understood what it was I needed to sell—a body that I would have to make not only functional but attractive. My goal was to create a presence—within myself if not within the world. Once that had been accomplished, I would be able to direct that presence at all that I pursued. I had a vague idea of "normalcy" in mind, I suspect, an idea that derived in part from seeing too many movies that depicted smiling, thriving American middle-class families at work and play, in part from an imagination which may have been hyperactive but still wanted all it had been taught to think it wanted. Is this really so overblown and childish a revelation as to make me blush with embarrassment today? It most certainly is.

Why do I, a man now in his sixties, still blush at my memories of being seventeen? The fact is that I succeeded in remaking myself. And success is normally what one is expected to be proud of. Perhaps I blush because I am a product of a pre-talk show America, where confession, if it had to be offered, was offered to God, and where a sense of decorum was still considered a public virtue. I feel awkward and shamefaced when I write about molding a physical self. And I find it far less difficult to write about the pain and hallucinatory nights of the onset of polio, how it felt to sense oneself on the threshold of death at the age of eleven, than I do to write about my own body's awakening. And this despite the fact that I am no longer seventeen, and that I no longer particularly care about my body's attractiveness. Today, bodies bore me—my own included.

Yet the process of remaking myself when I was a crippled adolescent taught me a great deal. It wasn't merely the bodily poses I went through, that I would see years later in the adolescence of my own sons. No, the adolescence of anyone struggling to take possession of his body lies beyond the usual male grunts and groans, the weightlifting and muscle flexing and concern with how one looks that afflict all boys as they move toward manhood. For me, there were no statements more important than the need to claim a physical presence. But in 1950, there were no examples for a cripple to follow. A good deal of what I learned had to be self-taught. Since the lessons were there for the taking, I learned. And I created a physical presence out of the leavings of illness.

I learned that the mind and will are the most skilled of cosmetic surgeons, that they impose themselves on the body. I learned that no one knows more about compensation than those who must confront the future with a serious physical disability. I learned that the instinct for survival is as powerful and creative a force as poets and philosophers have been telling us for thousands of years. A few years later, when I finally read Emerson, all I could think of was that I already had lived so much of what he was telling me. His insistence on self-reliance affirmed the recognitions polio thrust upon me—that in the world of the cripple, it is the body's insistence that counts for something. And I learned that the act of creating one's physical presence out of a damaged body had rewards that went beyond even the pursuit of women.

One lifted weights, it turned out, not for the sake of the body but to affirm the physical rhythms of the life one was in the process of claiming. One walked mile after mile on a swing-through gait not to get to a particular place but to get beyond the limitations that had been imposed on the mind as well as on the body. One lay in pools of sweat not to demonstrate effort or to show that one had worked hard but to force motion to acknowledge the body one was laying claim to. It was as if sweat were the lubricant of life. But the most enduring lesson, the lesson I would carry through the rest of my life, was not that I had triumphed over the fears that plagued me but that the state of the mind was not merely a physical state.

And I also learned then that men and women are profoundly different in their approach to the body. Even an age rhetorically dominated by the politically correct, an age which seems to feel an almost physical revulsion at the idea that the differences between men and women count for something in this world, even in such an age permit me to admit that one of the lessons I learned as a cripple in pursuit of women was that women were less obsessed by and less involved with the body than men are. "Vanity," we should say, "thy name is man."

Of course, I cannot prove any of this. There is no proof. I can only draw upon my own personal experience—and that experience, I remind myself, is the experience of a man who has had to struggle for a physical presence in the face of crippling loss. I know how limited my own experience is, and I still remember how hungry I was for a physical life when my mind bulged with dreams of fair women and my soul was pumped up with the determination to create my new man. I could chip away at my body the way a sculptor chips at stone. But even as I did, I knew that the body I created had already been doomed to be less significant in the eyes of women than it would be in my own. One could pursue women down all the corridors of imagination and fantasy—and one still would meet one's own self.

"That is not what I meant at all," says Prufrock's lady to her terrified knight. "That is not it, at all." I'm not sure why, but as I worked to create a body for myself, it struck me that women are better able than men to accept physical disability as a part of who a person is. Significant, undoubtedly—but no more than a part of the whole. For women, the body is rarely the essential person, the center of being. What Erica Jong called "the zipless fuck" is a more detached voyeurism than men experience. Prufrock was cuckolded in imagination—the worst kind of cuckoldry, as "honest" Iago understood—yet he was never able to understand that it wasn't physical daring he lacked but a sense of his own body's reality. Eliot could be bawdy and titillating, yet he never managed to come to terms with the truths of his own body. And he never pursued women to the point where he met himself.

In the pursuit of women, the lessons I absorbed were rarely dramatic. Only it was my own excessively dramatic expectations that lay in ambush for me, to threaten my dreams of emergence into the physical world. What is it that men want from women? An ease of conscience, a soothing of ego, a gesture of kindness. I think back to a warm summer evening soon after I had completed my junior year in college. I was crossing Broadway with my date, the same woman I was to elope with in another four years. We were hurrying to get to a play before the curtain went up. I wish Freud's ghost had been with me when I tripped and went sprawling. If he were, I wonder what he would have said about what it is that women want when he saw Harriet lean down, pick up one of my crutches, and hand it to me, even as, livid with rage, I pulled myself erect with my manly and violated arms. "You fell," Harriet said, the crutch like an offering between us. Nothing more—just, "You fell." The right words, as precise as even Freud could have wished. And the kind of response which took the wind from my sails, the rage from my soul, and left me feeling helpless in that physical being I had worked so long and hard to create—just another man who fell.

10

WONDER WOMAN
IN THE LAND OF
GOOD AND PLENTY:

BIG WINNERS AND LITTLE LOSERS

''THERE ARE no winners in this world," my Uncle Moe used
to insist whenever I pestered him about the secrets of handicap-
ping horses and men and politicians, "only little losers." My uncle was a handicapper of considerable talent in a Bronx neighborhood that valued the skill and acumen of its gamblers. And at
ten, the age at which I remember pestering him most relentlessly, I took a certain reflected pride in his reputation. I knew
even back then that his was no more than a minor talent as the
world measured talent; yet it spoke of someone who possessed a
certain substance where horses and boxers and politicians were
concerned. To have earned a reputation as a man who could pick
winners was not trivial. And yet, perhaps because of his reputation as a man who had respect for the odds, my uncle could never
shake off the conservative instincts that stamp most gamblers.

When it came to the question of where he was going to put his
money, he was not a man who believed in systems. Sooner or
later, all gamblers lose more than they win. The odds simply dic-
tate that a smart gambler understands how much he will have
to pay for the value of his entertainment. All other benefits of

knowing the odds are accidental. In the last analysis, nature's diciness was the sole truth a man could depend upon.

Still, I continued to pester my uncle for his "secrets," convinced that he could help me work my way through a world that even a ten-year-old knew to be treacherous and mined with pitfalls. Only he would never give me those secrets, other than to insist that there was no fixed formula for figuring the odds. Instead, he would offer me what radio talk-show hosts like to speak of as a "lifestyle philosophy." I would be better off, my uncle told me, if I never gambled. For this world we lived in was the world in which there were "no winners, only little losers." And gambling was more pedestrian than I thought. "You'll go to college, Lennie. You'll study, learn. You'll get yourself a real profession. Make something of yourself."

But that wasn't the kind of wisdom I was seeking at ten. Not that I felt an overwhelming desire to understand the precise odds of everything I had to face as a young boy. But I pestered my uncle for the secrets of the odds because my true hunger was to know whether I myself was up to the mark. I wasn't concerned with betting on horses or boxers or deciphering local politicians ("sellouts," my uncle would call them, voice filled with contempt). Not really. What concerned me were the odds on my own future. I was, as all children are, in pursuit of an ultimate self. And in that pursuit, I modeled even my bodily postures and facial expressions on those comic-book heroes whose adventures I followed religiously—Captain Marvel, Captain America, and God knows how many other muscle-bulging caped bodies drawn from the fantasies of middle-aged cartoonists. These were the heroes who whirled through my imagination in gaudy comic-book colors, and I devoured every page on which they had been given life.

Like most children, I was unsure of where reality began and

fantasy ended. Had I been asked to choose between the woman I loved most passionately, Wonder Woman, and America's pinup of choice, the leggy Betty Grable, I would have pledged heart and soul to that comic-book goddess without hesitation. In 1943, I did not know whether Wonder Woman could be labeled either "big winner" or "little loser"—but I knew that she was what songs called "the girl of my dreams." At ten, sex was well beyond the boundaries of experience, but that didn't keep her Amazon body from kissing my two-dimensional dreams of comic-book consummation.

I don't think that ten-year-old boys were expected to know very much about what making love entailed back in 1943. In any case, I confess that I myself knew next to nothing about the subject. I had the anatomy more or less correct in my yearning for a comic-book princess. But, as in fairy tales in which frogs turn to princes, it was my own suspension of disbelief in which I had been caught up. Even when I turned eleven—a year that possessed great significance in a boy's knowledge of sex and anatomy—it was her lovely image, blue-black hair like erotic hay thrust against passions I knew were illicit, that I would envision in my fantasies of sex. In Wonder Woman's comic-book face and hair and breasts, I discovered the lingering perfumes of hope. And why not? Even a comic-book body can be made into flesh by an active imagination.

In another short and painful year, that dream of sex would be linked to my own physical struggle for survival, and my greatest worry would become whether the rest of my body was doomed to die as my legs had died. In the boy's ward of a rehabilitation hospital, I would learn that I could live as communal a life as I had lived in my Bronx neighborhood. The boys in that ward, all twenty-two of them, shared not only comic-book fantasies of sex but the prospect of a dubious future. Our job was to learn to live as cripples. And it was then that my uncle's advice really began to haunt me. Worse than anything else we boys experienced in that ward was that none of us knew what was expected of cripples in a world by which, despite its sanctimonious piety, we had already been branded "life's losers."

The boys in that ward ranged in age from nine to thirteen, and we shared physical pain and bodily humiliation—spinal taps, bedpans, useless limbs—as well as fantasies of sex and resurrection. Fortunately, in that pretelevision world, we also shared a Friday night movie. It was at those weekly movies that I think I first began to understand why I loved Wonder Woman with such passion. By then, I knew more about anatomy and sex than I had when I lived among the normals in the Bronx. (One of the few positive aspects of illness is that it allows even children a more intimate relationship to their bodies.) More than Betty Grable's legs or Rita Hayworth's succulent red lips, Wonder Woman's comic-book body promised that what I was hungry for was what she could provide me with—the courage to endure.

Exactly why that courage should be modeled by a cartoon Amazon is still a mystery. There were other models I might have chosen. Why, for example, didn't I take my own grandmother as a model of the courage to endure? In her mid-seventies the summer I took sick, my grandmother, like many other ageless immigrant women, had been born with the capacity not only to make her fierce judgments but to carry them out. She faced God and man with neither tact nor equivocation. And if hers was the bravado of an old Jewish woman who simply did not know any better, that was already attractive to me before polio took me down. Yet I didn't choose my grandmother. Instead, I chose my comic-book Diana who was neither flesh nor blood but a cartoonist's two-dimensional idea of beauty and power. For me, she embodied the courage of women. She had grace, glamour, and beauty.

In the Land of Good and Plenty, my goddess reigned in spirit and in comic-book flesh.

Looking back, it is curious that my grandmother, always a magical being in my eyes and seemingly beyond ordinary flesh and blood, was not my model of power and courage. One of my vivid memories is of how she stood up to an unshorn collie that had gone mad with the heat one scorching July afternoon during the summer I was eight. The collie was running up and down the street, nipping every child and adult in sight. Along with two friends, I fled to where my grandmother was sitting, reading the *Vorwarts*. My grandmother simply stood up as the dog barked, holding her rolled-up Yiddish newspaper in the air as she firmly commanded the dog to leave her grandson alone. Crazed with heat, the collie paused, stared at her, panting, then turned and went off to nip at other heels until his owner finally collared him. My grandmother returned to reading the paper, as if nothing had happened. But it seemed to me, as it did to my friends who had also sheltered themselves behind her, that my grandmother had imposed her will on that crazed dog because she herself was a force of nature.

Yet it was not my grandmother's courage I sought. Nor was it Franklin Delano Roosevelt's, though he was always being peddled to us by the nurses and doctors as an example of what a crippled boy could do in spite of. . . . (We were expected to fill in that "in spite of" for ourselves.) To some extent, we boys did look to Roosevelt, whose power as president hinted at the possibility that the future might not be quite as unlivable as we thought. Yet truth will out—and the truth is that it was my vague sexual fantasies that inspired my passion for a comic-book Amazon. She fueled my desire to make myself over. I write this a bit sheepishly, I confess. Yet truth, no matter how embarrassing, is always in order when it comes to the sources of one's courage or lack of courage. I couldn't turn to a grandmother who had been left untouched by this America even after twenty-five years. As for F.D.R., even a president who was, like me, a cripple was distant, whereas, comic-book cartoon though she was, Wonder Woman ruled over the Land of Good and Plenty. From there, she offered what I needed—the hope of matching her two-dimensional strength and courage with my own.

Memory may trifle with the way it actually was, yet I can still feel the attraction of those early erotic fantasies. A boy on the verge of adolescence can be horny even when illness makes him terrified. I was prepared to kiss death itself for my love's sake. My yearning was not for comic-book breasts nor for shield and buckler but for her bodily wholeness, her splendid health. The day would come when I knew that I could endure without legs but not without the courage to face up to the consequences of illness. That day was still in the future when I was in the ward, yet like any normal boy verging on adolescence I was a prisoner of my own need and insecurity. If it made sense to go to women for endurance and courage, and it did, then I would go to my comic-book goddess. Not a bad choice, as it turned out:

> Hesperus entreats thy light,
> Goddess, excellently bright.

Boys who come of age with so powerful an inspiration, even one pulled from the pages of comic books, do not need convincing that women possess courage.

I'm still not sure of why my passion for Wonder Woman was so strong. Perhaps it was simply that my imagination needed a savior who possessed the simple clarity of comic books. Did boys whose lives had not been changed by illness look to women as models of courage, too? It's not something men usually speak of, particularly today, when, despite our passion for gender equality women are still indicted for not soothing fragile male egos. The sense that women have stolen courage from men is rarely voiced directly, yet it stands behind all those magazines now marketed like different brands of deodorant to bewail the state of men in America. To read those magazines, even at random, is to see how deeply men yearn for the unbridled simplistic masculinity found in John Wayne's films. Testing the self with male bonding rituals is thrust before us like salvation's own finger food. It's as if the history of men in America were reduced to a dialogue between Robert Bly and Teddy Roosevelt, two perpetual Boy Scouts deep in the forest of the self. If T. R. were to be resurrected, he would be immensely pleased at how ritualized manhood in America again promises to be. Pressed to old myths, gender studies for men is our latest literary growth industry. Men are urged to reclaim courage. But from whom? And to what purpose?

Perhaps as the price of entry into the booming culture of victimization. For men are now urged to view themselves as victims. How curious a spectacle it is to watch angry boys storming off, like a losing college football team at half-time, eager to fight the gender wars during a time in which resentment has become the great male passion and accusation the most powerful male dream. As they stew in the imperfections of history, more and more men focus on what has been taken from them. The most painful resentment turns out to be that the courage to be men has been sacrificed. That is the itch beneath our manly skins, and we scratch at it, intent on peeling the detritus of loss even as we think in horror of the women who mock us.

Of course, it's not men alone who fight the gender wars in America. Both sexes have created a grammar of gender difference in which illusion struggles with expectation. Status, not masculinity, is what most men really grieve for, even as memory bends the knee to the illusory Edens of the past. Forget Iron John's campfire roasts in the dungeons of Bly's imagination. King Arthur is dead—and it's a good thing, too. Yet like small boys reluctant to leave the circus without one last look at the clown, men woo the past, seeking a simpler, more innocent world. No longer will the craggy face of the Marlboro Man urge us to take that first puff. No longer will that first bender justify a drunkenness that had to be public in order to be meaningful. Memory and embarrassment walk hand-in-hand, as men play the game of mannered nostalgia.

Yet having acknowledged that, one must also note that not even the most radical feminist in the land can deny that this is a particularly joyless time to be a man in America. Our burgeoning sense of an absence that we equate with injustice is to be seen in all those aging warriors seeking manhood's grail in initiation rites as embarrassing as anything Malory envisioned for Arthur and his knights. Faced with manhood's demands, not even our poets are satisfied any longer with mere words. Like novelists and ex-athletes, they, too, want to freeze time, to beat the bushes for Hemingwayesque fulfillment—rifle in hand, foot on the carcass of the dead lion, eyes on the Hollywood horizon.

It isn't difficult to understand why the New American Masculinity possesses appeal. American men simply want to be braver than they are. And as with any movement in which gender or race or ethnicity is the principal currency, the kind of male psychobabble that is supposed to bond us creates a painful if comic self-consciousness. Yet the rhetoric of male bonding, however puerile it seems, does speak to why men still find the idea of manhood appealing. In a time in which they have been unable to assume traditional roles, men are eager to seize the sense of victimization for their own. And why not? For better or worse, the need to see the self as victim is incorporated into the politics of gender. And the difficulty we have with such politics is that it fortifies the worst impulses of a culture in which reality is primarily personal. Virtual Reality is, in fact, the reality we prefer in today's America, the most fertile ground for what small children still call "make-believe" the Western world has known. Our images of masculinity have so little to do with our actual experience that they are mind-boggling. We embody military valor in a movie star who did everything he could to keep out of the service during the greatest war in the nation's history; our newspapers and airways are filled with passionate debate about whether or not some whining overpaid athlete can be called a "real hero"; we use a vocabulary in which language is reduced to emotion and emotion to the utility of a label. In all these ways, men surrender to a Virtual Reality in which the times prove dangerous even when they lack danger, as we move beyond the need to do the world by the numbers.

Curiously enough, it is a lesson few men master, even when armed with the rhetoric of the men's movement. For stalking the numbers is one of the most intimate of masculine obligations. From childhood, American men are taught to measure themselves against others in competitions in which the numbers not only dominate but frame argument. Young boys compress their idea of manhood into opinion surveys in which they are asked to check themselves against the status of other boys (who have, of course, also been defined by the numbers). In place of character, we offer addition and subtraction. Our passions are reduced only to measurement, our manhood to image and statistics.

It has always been by the numbers that men in America have defined themselves, as if each of us harbors a collective idea of living unfettered by the actual past. Genteel and gentile, Eliot's Prufrock measured out his life with coffee spoons. The boys I came of age with in the rich ethnic stew of New York changed only the instruments of measurement. We did our lives by the numbers. With numbers, we defined everything from penis size to how many manhole covers one could hit in stickball. The length of an automobile, the inches of muscle in biceps and chest, the size of one's palm and the size of one's hat—all done by the numbers. Had he been born in the Bronx, poor Prufrock would also have sought numerical confirmations of existence, just another bright boy dropping his IQ number into the honey pot licked by all the nerds, flaunting his intelligence as if it were the price of the ticket. There, Prufrock would not have mourned his incapacity; rather, he would have figured out just how much money the Michelangelo the women in the room were talking of might bring at auction.

Bred to a world in which even the games boys played pressed statistic upon statistic, numbers endowed the hungers and aspirations we grew up with. I knew the earned run average of every pitcher on the Brooklyn Dodgers in 1943 as well as I knew exactly how many dollars Manhattan Island cost the Dutch in 1624. If boys today are more apt to know how many points per game Michael Jordan averages than the name of the nation's vice-president, that indicates only that the games have changed. The numbers still define us, an emotional Cartesianism we have learned to live with almost from infancy. The message remains in the numbers. To add, subtract, and multiply is our way of saying, "Therefore, I am."

But courage was never by the numbers. Courage was much too intangible. It was not something either man or boy could measure. If examples of it abounded, none was more accessible than the courage of women.

/ / /

Her name is not important. Not that I am ignorant of it. As names go, hers was simple enough. Judy Taylor. A name that counts as much as any name can. Names possess context not in themselves but in the ways we fuse them to time and place. It doesn't matter that, when I first met her, she was Judy Taylor and that when I met her again she had been turned into Judy Taylor Gentile. It was the same woman, the same tough human being. All that I am uncomfortable about at this point is that I remain much more certain of what her name was than of when we met. Was it the fall of 1970? Or the spring of 1971? Not knowing disturbs me, although I'm not, to be honest, certain of why. Even when I met her shouldn't matter. History was never the issue where Judy was concerned.

What matters is the letter I received in which she asked me to speak to an organization of physically handicapped men and women in Michigan. I no longer remember the name of that sponsoring organization, but Judy wanted me as its speaker because when she was a student she had read an essay I wrote which argued that those of us who were crippled should be urged to emulate blacks in making demands on an America willing to sentimentalize us but not willing to recognize our existence. Like much of what I wrote years ago, I find "Uncle Tom and Tiny Tim" embarrassing to reread today. The analogy between cripple and black now seems much too facile, while my impassioned vision of an integrated future for the races has been mocked by what we have made out of race in this nation. Yet I am still grateful to that essay, for it brought me in touch with one of the truly courageous people it has been my good fortune to know.

It's curious to write that about a woman I saw only two times in my life. We corresponded for some years after my talk to that organization in East Lansing, but we had been out of touch for at least fifteen years when she telephoned me in the fall of 1991.

Once again, Judy wanted me to be a speaker. Now working as the student counselor to handicapped students at Michigan State, she asked me to speak at a university weekend that was intended to celebrate "diversity" in the academic world. Despite my growing doubts about what I had heard more and more colleagues refer to as "the diversity business," I knew that I would agree to speak when I heard that thin reedy voice laugh and say, "I'm offering you the chance to be Michigan State's official university cripple."

She was now married, to a man who had lost control of a motorcycle and thus entered the shadowy world Judy had called home for her entire life. It was a marriage that affirmed what cripples learn early on: spasms of ill luck and poor fortune embrace the best and brightest, the common and ordinary. A motorcycle can be transformed into an electric wheelchair in a psychological economy where big winners become little losers in the blink of an eye. Judy would arrange for me to be housed at the university for the weekend, and she would see to it that her husband met me at the airport in his wheelchair-modified van. Would I please come to their house for lunch? "I'm Judy Taylor Gentile now," she said. "What's in a name?" Her laugh was a giggling cough, but it was an entry into her pride and pleasure at having made a life for herself. She was counselor to disabled students at the university, she was married, she was the mother of an adopted daughter in a wheelchair.

East Lansing had been an Oldsmobile city when I spoke there twenty years earlier, still loyal to the memory of Walter Reuther and still dependent upon G.M. But by 1992, it was just like any other university town, the kind of place in which women looked harshly at acquiescence to patronymic form. Judy was a staunch feminist. But she was also a cripple, and labels do not have much to do with the everyday problems we cripples are asked to focus

on. Her concern could not be on what one called a physical condition but on the acts her small, misshapen body demanded of
her every day. She had no choice but to press courage to need.
Where survival is concerned, patronymic form is rarely an issue.
Only those who are able to live in normal circumstances, with
normal bodies, can afford to think of it as an issue.

In a culture that likes to pretend to be classless, the cripple's
life is as close to a class issue as America can admit to. If his
body is crippled, even a Rockefeller will be a cripple first and a
Rockefeller second. To be crippled is beyond the name game, a
condition that does not change merely because one calls himself
"differently abled" or "handicapped." To be a cripple is to acknowledge that the future is to be defined by the diseases of the
past. The Judy Taylor Gentile at whose house I ate lunch in April
1992 was now a woman in her forties, but she still looked like
the college sophomore I had met twenty years earlier. Her face
seemed sculpted by illness, and her body seemed fastened to a
wheelchair that was as much part of her as her nose or eyebrows.
Judy possessed that chair—and was, in turn, possessed by it. It
was as if the chair were part of her presence, as if she had transformed a wheelchair into her own personal emblem, a triumph
of necessity.

> The barge she sat in, like a burnished throne
> Burned on the water

Like all who struggle with disease, Judy learned that only after
she had earned the trust of language would she be able to trust
reality. Like Caliban on his island, her condition enveloped her
dreams of emergence—for to select from dreams was to trust the
language of those who were normal, to place illusion in the service of resurrection. Like a throne burning on the water, a wheelchair could define time and create presence. From the window

of imagination, one could seize a sense of the world. Yet there are some realities that not even poetry can change. From infancy on, Judy had been forced to recognize certain simple facts. A wheelchair was not a metaphor. And disease was definition. In being crippled, one assumed a citizenship that had been painfully earned and dearly paid for.

Yet even in so painful a citizenship, one may discover that the crippled self is insufficiently crippled. The same gender politics that makes a man or woman insufficiently black or insufficiently Native American or insufficiently Asian can make us insufficiently crippled. At Michigan State's celebration of diversity, I watched as the melting pot melted into its own potential civil wars. That Judy was aware of such dangers was evident when she asked me to make myself available to a young Hispanic student she had been counseling. Like the two of us, he was in a wheelchair. At a reception of the groups that made for university diversity, I saw his brooding body maneuver in its chair, his darkly handsome face etched in a sneer framing lips and thin mustache against a pretense of worldliness he had not yet earned. An automobile accident had cost him his legs. Paraplegia filled him with rage, and Judy was trying to get him to make that rage "work for him."

But he had not yet learned his place in America. Arriving at college with the belief that his identity could be grounded in his being Hispanic, he learned that to be Hispanic could only take him so far. A week after his arrival, he joined one of the Hispanic student clubs on campus. But he was rejected. "We got to show them Anglos that Hispanics are strong," the club president told him. "How can I think of you as strong if you're in a wheelchair?"

Not particularly subtle. But not illogical either. As free in

mind as she was twisted in body, Judy was not one to deny entrepreneurial logic when she had to confront it. The body impresses
even the normals. And we cripples know, as well as anyone can,
that courage begins with the body and that the body is the source
of our need for courage. In the name of the group, the courage of
individuals can be mocked. For group pride—*all* group pride—
is bombastic rhetoric intended to minister to the victim in his
victimization. Yet as Orwell showed in *Animal Farm*, some victims are worthier than others. With diversity, issue is less important than image. What counts is establishing oneself as victim. Those of us doomed to the mundane fact of being crippled
discover that we cannot compete with victims who have drama
and/or prurience on their side. Rapists, child molesters, and
peeping Toms entertain the nation on daytime talk shows. With
such richness, to be a cripple is a pedestrian kind of victimization. "Nature loves to hide," remarked Heraclitus. And nature
sometimes chooses to hide behind suffering. The Hispanic students in that club had their own sense of what was to be their
proper destiny. A man in a wheelchair was not strong. What they
sought was the image of Che succored by wily, determined peasants. And peasants do not use wheelchairs. Besides, what other
use do the strong have for the weak if they cannot serve as
symbols?

In her politics, Judy was still pretty much where she had been
in the 1970s, an unreconstructed believer in the need for govern-
ment to right the balance. Not even Senator Dole of Kansas,
withered right hand as symbolic in its way as that Hispanic student's wheelchair, could have kept so tough a woman at arm's
length. Judy had no use for the rhetoric of personal responsibility
Americans have grown so fond of over the past two decades. A
woman who had earned her anger, she needed no lectures on the
cost of freedom. Or any pep talks on forging her own destiny. She

had no use for that self-consciously steely John Wayne guts and glory rhetoric, for she had already paid the price demanded of speech. And she would not have fit very well around a campfire with overgrown boys discussing the cost of courage. No matter what price she had paid, Judy knew that she had only gotten to where she could never rest securely anyway.

Only what I remember best about her has little to do with politics. What I remember is that voice. It wasn't a pleasant voice and it wasn't a tough voice—but it was a voice that brooded with anger for a world she had not made yet had been forced to live in. One heard in its broken timbre the tones a brave individual had created for herself. It made me remember the sound of voices I had heard some years back, in Israel, if only because it refused the victim's cry those voices were filled with. My wife and I had gone to visit Rachel's Tomb in Bethlehem. As we stood, tourists properly deferential, at the rear of the tomb, three Moroccan Jewish women began to ululate in front of the tomb as their bodies swayed to a verbal unison of that terrifying sound cutting through the cool morning Bethlehem air like a snaking whip. So harsh a music, I thought, might bring tears to God's very own eyes. Wrapped in chadors, the three women wailed. They were barren, our guide explained, and thus they swayed before Mother Rachel, begging her to intercede with God and grant them children. The scene was as close to a Jewish version of what Reinhold Niebuhr called Catholic "Mariolatry" as I could think of. So total was their grief, so absolute their surrender to Mother Rachel, that I felt as if I were intruding on a private conversation among maniacs. As they howled, I turned my wheelchair around and fled Rachel's Tomb, as if there were a danger that my own body and soul could be violated by the grieving supplicants.

Judy's voice was the very opposite of those howling women. I never heard it wail or beg. Instead, it seemed to hover in the air, like a wounded bird. Judy's pride was never to beg—not from man, and not from God, either. Her voice was weak and reedy—but singular and distinctive, too. Unlike voices that beg, hers was a voice that demanded. As American, in its way, as the voice Fitzgerald spoke of as "full of money." Judy's voice did not jingle with wealth, as Daisy Buchanan's did. Nor was it given its tone by allure or success or power. It was not the voice of a woman who shops in Bergdorf or Nieman Marcus or Tiffany's. It was a voice filled with pain and effort and the knowledge of how much a lifetime of defiant courage had cost its bearer.

And it was the voice of a woman who still insisted upon her right to define life for herself in a country which asked of its cripples perpetual beggary. Watch Jerry Lewis' next telethon if you need a reminder of how, like after-dinner mints, Americans want their stories of pain and suffering spicy enough to tingle yet sweet enough to swallow. Victims in America are defined by the dysfunctional notes of their songs. Which American is willing to admit that the luck of the draw has gone against him? If one chooses to be a victim, one must make one's pain accessible. A voice full of money calls up not Judy's twisted body but the slender grace of ownership that Fitzgerald bestows upon Gatsby's sexless love. Money is a dinner bell in the voices of the rich, commanding, imposing order. Those wailing women in front of Rachel's Tomb had sounded the victim's song out of need. In Judy's reedy voice, one detected a different call—a brave woman's insistence that she would resist fate down to her dying breath.

Tell me that it is better for men to search for courage in those pup tents of boyhood fantasy where Faulkner's ageless bear trees one's soul. Tell me that and I will remind you of what my gambler uncle understood so well—that in the country of the mind, there are no winners, only little losers. Freud, who knew more about pain and courage than it is fashionable to admit today, must have had something similar in mind when he shrugged off a friend's praise of Franz Rosenzweig for insisting on doing his work despite a ravaging illness. "What choice does he have?" the old cigar-smoker asked. Had she heard that remark, Judy would have winked, then agreed with Freud in her reedy voice.

She died less than a year after that diversity weekend. Her husband phoned to tell me that her end had come. As suitable an end as man or woman can expect, I suppose. She struggled, she fought, she made a few more claims on what must have been, by then, nothing more than her battered will to resist. If a lifetime as a cripple taught her nothing else, it taught her that she could resist the demands of pain and illness by affirming not life in general but her own life in particular. Give in and you are dead. It really is that simple.

For a woman who possessed her own lifelong citizenship in the country of the crippled, I suspect it was important to meet her end well. Pain writes our true memoirs, and the competition for its prizes remains fierce. In the Land of Good and Plenty, so many little losers are alive and well. But Judy is dead. I make no claim that the manner of her dying will teach the rest of us some valuable lesson. I do not believe that we learn from the examples of others. Yet in a nation which more and more worships power and wealth and celebrity, I think hers is a better example of human possibility than all the childish rituals urged upon men today. No campfires. No myths. No bonding. Just the refusal to resign the self to its death. And the insistence on the body's struggle, a struggle that teaches us that even when we triumph, it is for the briefest of moments and for the most narrow of choices. That, one hopes, is lesson enough for all of us.

11

NAMING
NAMES

THE TELEPHONE'S repeated rings hover in the air like some audio courier whose arrival and departure run through imagination even before he makes his presence known, an abusive alarm sounding depths the passing of time cannot sound by itself. By now, the sound is a ritual. When I hear it, I can feel my body tense up, the muscles of forearms and shoulders seemingly wired tight enough to strum. Irritated at the prospect of once again hearing his voice hammer against the fragments of a past he insists on sharing with me, I take another deep breath. I need to stay in control. Like a top sergeant addressing a new batch of enlistees, I command myself, speaking aloud. "Do not pick the telephone up! Under no circumstances are you to pick the telephone up."

Not for his ringing summons. Not again. I have already talked to him three times this morning, and I do not trust myself to pick the telephone up once more. Having been shaped by my own illness, I think that I have the right to refuse being shaped by his. Only I can already feel the bitter anguish of anticipation wringing my heart. His voice is an apparition filling the room with a ghostly presence. I sense it hiding inside the ringing telephone—his disease, sitting here, alongside me. Staring dead ahead at the white wall of my bedroom, I say, "I am not going to pick it up. Not again. Not this time." The words are directed at the wall. The wall says nothing back.

Only the ringing continues. And even though I close my eyes and repeat aloud my determination not to pick the phone up, the ringing does not allow me to ignore the shrill terror with which it punctuates this late morning light. Enraged as much by my own reluctance to break this freeze created by the ringing as by the prospect of speaking to him, I finally force myself to lift the receiver from its cradle. His will has beaten mine. He has pushed me to the point where I must recognize my own cowardice. Aware of defeat at his hands, I feel like a child who suddenly wants to reformulate the rules of the game. Anger envelops me, as I tell myself that I can still beat him if I disguise my voice. As if it were possible to fool a man who has known me since the day of my birth almost six decades ago. For the voice is the voice of my Uncle Moe. And the hand that picks the phone up is the hand of his caretaker, my hand.

"Hello," I say, gruffly.

"The Polish Prime Minister!" my uncle's voice shouts into the phone, welcoming his triumph without even bothering to acknowledge my "hello." "I got to remember his name, Lennie. The one that played the piano."

I close my eyes as a tremor of anger, as pure as an icicle, stirs my body. I am being used by my uncle, and I hate being used. But I must not tell my uncle about my anger, I remind myself. I cannot explode so that my uncle will know how much I feel the humiliation of the way his aging fixations insist upon a nephew's intercession. "Paderewski," I hear my voice say, after a long pause. "Ignace Paderewski." I sigh. Then, as gently as I can, I add, "I've already told you that three times this morning, Uncle."

"Paderewski!" my uncle cries. An excited cry of triumph, a cry in which I hear the edge of terror slip from his voice and momentarily spin from his mind. His triumph is tempered by relief, as if a troublesome boil has at last been lanced. The voice softens now, as my uncle continues, "He was Prime Minister when we left for America. When I was twelve. Did I ever tell you that, Lennie? That he was prime minister."

"Ten times since yesterday afternoon, Uncle," I answer. Exasperated, I realize that my eyes are still closed, as if my burgeoning anger can control the world I must live in simply by blocking out the sight of what it has become for my uncle. Yet as angry as I am with him because of his persistence, I know that the greatest portion of the anger I feel must be directed at me. My uncle has the desperate daring of obsession, while all I have is the excuse of cowardice. He is old and dying—and I am in the service of his passing.

"I'm sorry," he says. The apology, equally inevitable, is another ritual. He offers it as if the words had been precast, configured to the depths of our mutual need. This time, it is my uncle who sighs, a sigh that is an offering to me, a gift of his need for reconciliation, a sign that he is now ready to apologize—in his fashion. "I don't mean to bother you so much, Lennie. Only I can't help myself. You should understand, I can't help myself. It's like bees buzzing in my head."

He is sorry and I am angry and ashamed and humiliated and half-crazed with guilt and irritation and disgust. All right—disgust with myself more than with him. But I cannot, must not, tell him any of this. He reacts to my anger the way I myself used to react to the anger of adults—teachers, parents, even strangers—when I was five or six, with a sense of naked terror that the world had suddenly lost its balance and was threatening to come crashing down around me. My uncle is working his way back into that childhood he thought he had left in the Poland of the pianist prime minister. He has cast aside all thought of the courage men need to face the end in order to become just another aging supplicant, one more beggar for the kindness and understanding and forgiveness of his caretaker. That his caretaker is his nephew is of little importance. I could be a visiting nurse or the doctor he has been seeing for thirty-five years. I could be an old friend from the fur market who has traveled up to the North Bronx to see him. "It's okay," I say. And with that, I am finally able to open my eyes. "Call any time you want, uncle," I add, resignedly. "It's okay."

"Thank you, Lennie," he says. Then we say good-bye, both his apology and my shame tempered by our mutual recognition that, at some time during the next half hour, the telephone may very well ring again and my uncle's voice will once more war with time's passing as I hear him demand, "The Polish Prime Minister! The one that played the piano. What's his name again? I can't remember his name!"

For my uncle, the past is ever watchful. At eighty-three, he suffers from more ailments than either of us could have envisioned years ago. His heart, his eyes, his urinary tract, his prostate. His body is a decaying medicine chest of illness and of wear and tear. Most of all my uncle suffers simply from sitting in his apartment in the Norwood section of the Bronx, naming names, another Adam in the Garden of Memory. He is alone in that apartment now, other than a woman from Jamaica whom I pay to care for him. Like the rest of a man's life, a ritual into death and dying, is his being taken care of. Each Friday, I drive to the apartment house in the neighborhood where my uncle and Elaine, his caretaker, now live. I briefly talk to her about how my uncle feels, as if he were still a man whose life was open to ordinary sensations and ordinary comings and goings. Every week, she tells me that my uncle is fine. "Sharp as a tack," she says, in her soothing Jamaican accent. And every week I thank her, as we both pretend that my uncle is still the man I knew all my life—horse player, gambler, trade unionist. A mensch. A man among men.

I, too, once lived in that apartment house. When I was a child. And when I drive up there I check first to see that the name "Niles Gardens" is still discernible in the stone lintel above the entrance. It is a house that holds part of my past, too. I try not to look at anything else, just that name cut in stone. I honk the car horn and Elaine comes downstairs and we talk about my uncle and she invariably tells me he is "sharp as a tack" and I hand her weekly payment to her and then I thank her for taking care of my uncle and even as she turns to walk back inside Niles Gardens I gun the car motor, eager to leave this street and my uncle behind me as quickly as possible.

I never go upstairs to see my uncle when I drive to Rochambeau Avenue. I am in a wheelchair now and there are five marble steps inside the lobby that one must climb in order to get to the elevator. Even if I could still climb those stairs, the elevator is more often than not broken. It doesn't matter. My uncle never leaves the apartment. And he never comments, not even over the telephone, on his nephew's inability to go upstairs. He is satisfied with a caretaker nephew who is no more than a voice on the telephone. And yet, for my uncle, that telephone voice is a constant source of clarification, an electronic connection to a world to which he no longer belongs—and that no longer belongs to him.

His sister and brothers and brother-in-law are dead. Other than me and my cousin Leo, who lives on Long Island and who drives into the city to see him every other week, his other nephews and nieces are scattered from Boston to Memphis. They, too, are voices on the phone, given visible shape and substance only on the rare occasions when they return to New York. Their names, like mine, are now linked to the electronic hookup of the world.

But neither their names nor mine are the names my uncle is searching for. No, the names he seeks so desperately from the past reflect his own haphazard assault on the tyranny of the present. Drab and forlorn and unshaven, my uncle seeks to reify everything that he can remember. And so it is that he must weigh down each name with a significance he alone can understand. He throws those names at me and at my brother and at my cousins and at his grand-nephews and grand-nieces as if the only affirmation of existence he can still make is to call them up and parade them for our admiration, random jottings from the storehouse of his memory.

"There was this second baseman for the Dodgers. During the war, when you got the polio, Lennie. What was his name? Tell me his name." Even if I cannot win at my uncle's frantic version of Jeopardy, I am expected to absorb his rage at not being able to remember the name of that second baseman, a rage that can so easily transform him into a petulant child. For my uncle's urgent preoccupation with the past consists not only of remembering those names but of reliving the life they have defined, his life, for the past ten years. Their names frame his world even as they testify to his past existence. And their names speak of the only syllogism with which my uncle can still affirm his existence. "I remember, I was there." At eighty-three, alone and waiting for the end to swallow up even the names by which he still defines the man he was, my uncle defends his existence, verbally bobbing and weaving like the fighters he taught me to admire when I was a child, trying to avoid that final beating, the last threat, the end to memory.

There may be others in this world who can invoke a wartime utility infielder for the Brooklyn Dodgers ("the Brooklyns," is what my uncle still insists on calling them) named Eddie Basinski and a tough Bronx middleweight named Steve Belloise and the first woman appointed to a cabinet position, Frances Perkins, and the great leader of the coal miners' union, John L. Lewis ("the only Republican," my uncle insists, "ever worth a damn"). But not the way my uncle invokes them—with the strident demand that each name, valiantly pulled from memory's bank, sustain the dying self in its multiplicity of needs. For that is what my uncle seeks from the names he hurls against me and against this world. Those names are a conglomeration of stars, pinpoints of lights dotting a universe he is afraid to leave. And he must ricochet like a jackhammer out of control between the ghosts of his European childhood and the ghosts of his recent American past. Those names define both world and time, and only those names, like ranked sentinels, still tell him that what was once real must forever remain real.

"Only connect!" said E. M. Forster. A line that writers such as my uncle's caretaker nephew love to quote. We probably quote it too often. Now I wonder whether E. M. Forster, too, was simply trying to soothe some old relative waiting to die. Words may be dumdums. But names are the bullets of reality.

Did E. M. Forster ever harangue himself with a name like Mushy Callahan? "He was a convert, Lennie. The bastard, he was geshmat. His real name, it was Morris Scheer. An East Side boy. He turns Catholic and then he fights Jackie Kid Berg and Jackie beats him for the title. They called this Berg 'the Whitechapel Whirlwind.' Because he was an English Jew. And because it's in England, this here Whitechapel."

It is the names on which he depends to connect himself to

himself, to his past, to the death he both fears and longs for. All those names promise to structure time again. Jackie Kid Berg is the Whitechapel Whirlwind, Mushy Callahan was born Morris Scheer, Beau Jack was called the Georgia Shoeshine Boy. Names, names, and more names. Bodies reduced to names. Lives kissed by names. In death, nothing will exist but names. And no reality will be greater than those names that define him.

The next day, he telephones me at my office, bullying the graduate student who answers the phone by insisting that it is absolutely imperative, a matter of life and death, that he be allowed to speak to me. I frown when the student stands at the door of my office to inform me that my uncle is on the phone. Zhengming is from China, and he has never heard of Beau Jack or Mushy Callahan or Jackie Kid Berg, the Whitechapel Whirlwind. But I have this idea that the Chinese, like the Jews and Italians who once lived in my old neighborhood, have been raised to revere the aged. I have the idea that all old people possess a touch of the holy as far as Zhengming is concerned. I wonder whether the Chinese welcome being weighed down by their old. I do not think Zhengming ever would allow himself to feel the irritation I feel. Yet even as I acknowledge my guilt, I know that I do not want to respond to this latest call. I will not respond, I tell myself, frowning. In the doorway, Zhengming smiles, then shrugs. I shake my head.

Only that is when the warning light flashes in my mind. This may be the emergency my imagination dreads. Heart, lungs, broken bones—each and all threatens to unleash an old man's life from its moorings. I sigh. Then I pick the phone up. Just as I suspected, it turns out to be none of these. "An actor," my uncle offers eagerly, not even bothering to apologize for telephoning me at the office. "Clint somebody. I remember he did this Western on television. Years ago. *Cowhide*, I think it was called. Or something like that. Please."

"Clint Eastwood," I say. "The show was called *Rawhide*."

"Clint Eastwood!" he echoes. "That's it. Clint Eastwood. *Rawhide*." Like a tire leaking air, I listen as his breath breaks the tension of expectation. Then he sighs. He understands that he can now offer the ritual apology. "I'm sorry I had to disturb you in your office, Lennie." Now that the question has been answered, the proprieties can be properly observed. "How are you feeling? How are the boys? How is Harriet?"

Other than these passing bursts of rage, which quickly turn into guilt and then into acceptable irritation, I cannot claim that my uncle's frenzied roll calls from his past affect me deeply. The names that mean so much to him are simply words to me. Yet when I pull back from my own involvement in what both of us know is his approaching loss of all consciousness and all names, I wonder whether there is something to his urgent need to recover those names that I do not fully understand. Perhaps naming names is not merely a way of holding onto the past but a preparation for letting go of it, a tribute to what gave my uncle's life definition and meaning, that made it *his* life.

Perhaps it is not the ghosts lingering in memory that he seeks to affirm as he burrows deeper within himself, forcing himself to name those names. Isn't it possible that what my uncle is really hunting for as he relentlessly prowls through memory for the names that anchor his past is the continuity that marks the life of a man as having been worth living, as still being a life that is definably his, even when it has been stamped with the performances of others.

"A fighter, Lennie," he pleads. "He lived somewhere in the neighborhood. Up near Reservoir Oval, I think is where he lived.

He tried to organize a boxers' union. I can't remember his name. I think he got this here Alzheimer's. What was his name, Lennie? What?"

I do not know that fighter's name. But as I listen to my uncle's voice trying to purge itself of the never-forgotten terror of forgetting, I envision my own face two decades into the future. A prospect that I will undoubtedly approach with my own fear and trembling. For I see a man who looks as withered and pained at eighty-three as my uncle's voice tells me he is now. My future, too, will be as the namer of names. And if I close my eyes, I can hear myself talking to one of my sons. It does not matter whether it is Mark or Bruce. All that matters is that we are talking over the telephone. Only the voice is mine now, and it is I who must name names, trying to barricade myself into the reality of the past, to keep that past from sliding off the face of the universe into the unacknowledged country before I myself pass through there. I hear myself speak, voice filled with the growing sense of danger of losing those names by which I measure my own life's passing. Will it matter whether I beg my son for the name of a Yankee right fielder who had a good arm or the name of that Italian prime minister murdered by terrorists or the name of a Soviet ballet dancer who defected to the West? It will not be their names I am searching for, just as it will not be their courage that I want him to affirm. It will be my own. And the desperate courage of my long-dead uncle.

12

FATHERS, SONS, BROTHERS, STRANGERS:

A MEDITATION ON COURAGE, MEMORY, AND BELONGING

I picture the equality which would then arise between us—and which you would be able to understand better than any other form of equality—as so beautiful because then I could be a free, grateful, guiltless, upright son, and you could be an untroubled, untyrannical, sympathetic, contented father. But to this end everything that ever happened would have to be undone, that is, we ourselves should have to be canceled out.

Kafka, *Letter to His Father*

SELF-PORTRAITS are rarely portraits of the self alone. For me, it is my younger brother in whose presence my own mask cracks. In a curiously intimate sense, my brother's life is where my own truest self stands revealed. And if Abe's life is not where I necessarily choose to begin, it is where I so frequently seem to end. Reflections upon the past's meaning, speculation about future possibilities—in the quest to frame a self, to see one's brother is to see oneself anew, alone in the nerve-jangling funhouse of imagination's eye.

/   / /

It is there, then, in my own raucous imagination, that I hear my brother, his sense of injustice clenched as tightly as a fist, pounding me until I feel like a cornered boxer with no place to hide. Through the telephone wires, the sullen imperatives of Abe's accusations demand recognition. He wants an older brother ready to acknowledge that *his* life was forced to accommodate itself to *my* illness. But what is it I can tell him that he does not already know? What defense do I offer for the course illness took? Do I say to him, "I know that disease is a sharing. Even between brothers? Especially between brothers." Do I announce that I realize a man should be able to chart both illness and courage on an emotional graph that traces their effects upon each other? I know that we are not speaking of abstractions here, that we are speaking of what occurred between us, between two men connected by blood and a shared past. Maybe I should respond to his anger with my own and demand that he check his facts, shout him down by reminding him that it was, after all, I who lost the use of my legs. I suppose that I could even give in to banality and apologize—simply say, "I'm sorry!" and put an end to it. Only all the weight of the evidence is on his side. Polio crippled me. But he paid so much of the price I should have paid.

And so I find myself listening to Abe's accusations as if I am caught up bodily in one of those black and white newsreels from the 1930s, the film so grainy that the tanks on screen look like wound-up toys rolling across patched and peeled terrain and death itself seems curiously mesmerizing. An end to questions offers the stamp of finality. Yet my brother's rage, as I imagine it, continues to hammer away at me. I wish I could attend to each shading of tone, to give each individual word, each angry syllable, a proper response. Only as Abe speaks of how much my being crippled cost his childhood and adolescence, I retreat into my own burgeoning resentment. His words rain down on me, yet all I can envision is a Chaplinesque newsreel in which Mussolini sneers with contempt for Ethiopia, hands on fat hips as he preens for the newsreel cameras. Snapping his fingers while strutting his stuff on the balcony, Il Duce's actor's courage offers itself to the frenzied Roman mob in the square below. How silly an image for a man trying to measure the truth of a brother's imaginary accusations. Only it can't be helped. The mind forces its images on brothers, just as it did on Cain when he wondered why Abel's sacrifice, and not his, had been found worthy in God's sight.

But I can't avoid my brother's accusations with remembered images of Il Duce on his balcony. The truth is that even in our imaginary confrontations, all I can do is to listen to my brother in silence—proof enough that deep down I believe he is right. Even if I were successful in hiding within that grainy old newsreel, I would not be able to change how right he is. Men are linked to each other, as both Christians and Marxists like to claim. If that is so, then to acknowledge a blood brother's rage is to acknowledge the most powerful of links. Disease *is* a sharing. My brother paid a terrible price for the polio that crippled me— an even higher price, I sometimes think, than the price I myself paid. Guilt is the anvil on which our links were forged, just as it is the syllogism on which we two have constructed the logic of our current relationship. I am not part of that 1930s Roman mob, nor am I an Ethiopian warrior about to hurl a spear against the steel skin of an Italian tank. I am a brother's brother, another American adrift in the 1990s, painfully aware of that time when he was my keeper. Neither of us can ever forget that. Pulled into a world where drama is played out not in public squares but in the dim confines of a Bronx apartment, I listen to my brother unfold his version of my life.

And if my life turned out to be his legacy, too, then why shouldn't he? In certain respects, the virus that took my legs took things of greater value from him—his childhood and adolescence. So that the mind's comedy, in which Il Duce berates the world from a balcony in Rome, is overwhelmed by the wrench of pain I hear in my brother's voice. Not our laughter at how absurd history's pomp and circumstance may be but our fear of the intimate legacies pain imposes on our relationship— that is what binds us to each other, as those same legacies bind us to the subtleties of a past whose love and bitterness we share. What I detect in my brother's voice, as it burns through the wires from Memphis, are the memories he earned. For men earn the memories that sustain them, just as they earn the roles they play—father, brother, husband, son. In imagination, I am condemned to listen to his words as they sting my flesh like pellets from a BB gun. I must look at the self my brother sees, in that landscape which, even as it grows distant, defines the man each of us has become. Only this time my search is not for what of myself I see back there. It is for what of my brother was left back there with me.

Both Abe and I have long since departed from the streets that framed our coming-of-age. After completing his graduate work in history at Duke, my brother settled in Memphis, capitol of that Deep South which was the *Gehenna* of our New York City childhoods. I traveled a much shorter road—at least as far as distance is concerned—to Manhattan, that spot on the map both Abe and I were conditioned to think of as "the real city." Yet the past that binds is also the past that separates. The question is not merely one of geography but of whose version of reality we can accept. Abe and I are not only brothers, we are also men trying to understand what formed us—each of us a husband, father, taxpayer, citizen. And each a son to that same dead father. As I listen to his voice fill with accusation, it occurs to me that my brother, like me, is middle-aged. The thought is so sudden that it shocks me, disintegrating time. I don't understand why that is so. Not really. I have no difficulty in accepting that my sons and my wife and I myself are growing older. But when I see Abe on his trips back to New York or on my own forays to Memphis, I am stunned to see that he has a beard now, gray and bushy, and that his face has taken on the contours of our father's face.

Like me, my brother is one of memory's children. Even in my imagination, he measures the rage in his heart by everything that lies unresolved in the past we mutually claim. Only it is his to interpret, he now insists, even more than it is mine. It is his past that we must decipher. When he speaks of his daughters, my nieces, or asks after his nephews, my sons, his focus is on the life we shared. In the depths of his own imagination, he believes that I still threaten the integrity of his past, that I may yet steal it from him as I stole his childhood and adolescence. That is the way brothers sometimes face each other, the past a possession to be fought over and struggled for, even as it anchors memory and accusation. Yet that is not what the past was supposed to do. The past was supposed to harbor our triumphs and tragedies, to shape what we would make of ourselves through a personal geography in which 206th Street's small apartment buildings and two-family "private" houses would stand to the end of consciousness like traps on a Monopoly board. Over there, an empty lot to be replanted as a Victory Garden during the early days of the war; across Rochambeau Avenue, the three schoolyards of P.S. 80 in which we played ball; up the avenue and around the corner, a cellar with lamps and an old couch that had been made into a "clubhouse," a dungeon to which one might bring a girl and one's hungers. Places of memory invite each of us to a still-passionate romance with all those urban places of the heart that can feed a man belief in his own value.

Only what anchors my brother and me even more firmly to our past is that father whom we each recall so vividly, that man whose hold on us, twenty years after his death, still reinforces the awkward simplicity of all that we seek. For the dead father belongs to each of us. He is Abe's father and mine, *our* father. And as his sons, we are even closer than we are as brothers, a truth we battle over as we speak across the thousand miles that separate us. What is it we speak of? About facing that narrow coil of memory where sons struggle with the desire to rearrange their lives and defy the lessons of time. Abe and I recognize that truth between us must be limited to what each of us can make his peace with. There are immigrant fathers, there are American sons—and there are the memories of those immigrant fathers that the American sons are condemned to live with. Scores of immigrant fathers who brought into this world scores of American sons. Yet neither of us can take solace from the knowledge that the condition is not ours alone.

We have our memories of the cost of the love that dead father commanded. But those memories are not the way it was supposed to be. In the movies, pipe-smoking Judge Hardy was our image of American fathers. Of course, we knew that the judge would have been out of place in so cramped an apartment as ours. In a New York tenement, his gentle advice would have been much more difficult to follow. And neither Abe nor I could compete with the American charm of a Mickey Rooney. We knew that, too. Finally, we knew that immigrant fathers did not give advice to American sons. Our job was to interpret the nation's ways for him. As for love, he had no choice but to assume that we would give to him what he so willingly gave to his own father in Galicia. That was a father's due in the Old Country, where even dead he commanded the love of a living son because such love was considered as natural as the phases of the moon. Here, we are the American sons—to the nation, not the man, born and bred.

In the tiny entrance foyer to a one-bedroom apartment, our father's father stares down at us from the wall. In the photograph, he looks much bigger than our father, his son, the walnut frame bordered by the cracked plaster of the foyer wall. A square skullcap sits on his head. He has a broad forehead, while the touch of a frown testifies to his high seriousness. I cannot think of him as my grandfather, yet he occupies a permanent place in my mind—not so much man as a mysterious presence working God's purpose. Or so our father, his son, insists. Only Abe and I see not God's purpose but a man able to command, a face capable of ordering around our father, who himself commands only my brother and me. Americans are supposed to think of themselves as born to command. Does that explain why each of our father's sons is secretly ashamed of the love he feels for him?

That is what I want to ask Abe. Only I am afraid of what his answer may be. His brooding sense of injustice sweeps past everything in its path, like a cyclone of retribution smashing against the reality we share, until, a bursting dam of pain and emotion, he himself is flooded by those moments with our father when he was forced to take my place. A core of resentment against which I offer only my rising irritation. The past a giant vacuum cleaner sucking each of us into its center. We are grown men, I want to say to my brother. Such memories are too trivial to serve as anchor for a man's life. Yet I listen and nod when the justice of an accusation hits home, as if my brother were sitting across from me at the kitchen table rather than speaking across those imaginary telephone wires from Memphis. It was he, Abe reminds me, the younger son by four years, who *davened* with our father in the synagogue at Yom Kippur. Time closes on the approach of evening like God's own bony fingers. "Me!" he insists. "Doing your job." But it isn't a question of who prayed with our father, I want to protest. I was "sick," and so he was expected to be both older *and* younger son. Only my brother still remembers, as if it were yesterday, the boundaries of obligation during the Days of Awe. His obligation, not mine.

Let him begin with beginnings, even if my defense proves inadequate. The Days of Awe were, for both my brother and me, not so much between God and man as between father and sons. It is not reality that proves disconcerting when prayer is remembered but the expectations to which prayer then gave voice. What was it our dead father expected his sons to atone for when our need was not for food to break the fast nor for the approval of our father's God but for him, for the dead father himself, to tell us once again that we were good sons, American sons? His need for the comfort of belief was what we wanted to satisfy even if we remained beyond belief's comfort. For his belief threatened to condemn us to that dark Europe of his superstitious longing. The legacy of American sons was to extol the immigrant father, and then refuse to follow him.

Yet if I did not follow him, I never adequately praised that man who was not able to seize the America his sons hungered for. Twenty years after his death, how can I speak of the courage of a fear-filled immigrant without sentimentality? How do I explain that he blessed America as savior even as he cursed his inability to understand it? Did either Abe or I have any choice but to reject our father—with love, yes, but reject him nonetheless? He never understood the country of our liberated imaginations, and we felt nothing but contempt for his Europe. Not for us Emma Lazarus' passionate plea. If we wanted Europe's tired and poor or those huddled masses yearning to breathe free, all we had to do was take a good look in the mirror.

> *Mirror, mirror, on the wall*
> *Who's the greatest success of them all?*

Not our immigrant father. Sons want more than a sigh of resignation in the bleak night, or a shrug of the shoulders to indicate that the father accepts his fate. What our father could not understand was that the laconic acceptance his sons found in Jimmy Stewart's voice echoed immensities of space that could never be filled, a majestic American emptiness so far beyond the Yiddish inflections of our father's shtetl past that it made us wince at the thought of what he must sound like to the Irish on our block who had assumed the title (if not the prerogatives) of the neighborhoood's "real" Americans. We did not want the puffiness and raw nerves of Galicia. We did not need the sweaty smell of bodies laboring or the cloaked consciousness by which pogroms were dated. We had no use for the endless recitations of death and destruction, anniversaries in which catastrophe was hysterically pledged to memory. What we wanted were fireworks on the Fourth of July, eating hot dogs at Coney Island, belly whopping on our sleds on Mosholu Parkway's hills in winter's snow. The places we hungered for were incalculably beyond his unquestioning loyalty to a God who commanded that the heart of the ghetto beat to the rhythm of old fears. America asked of its sons only the courage to change. Of its immigrant fathers, it asked nothing.

He possessed a different kind of courage from what America wanted—quiet, weathered, dull. There was little in Fred Kriegel that one could speak of as daring. Even his stories about the Old

Country downplayed man in favor of that tough God who seemed to challenge his endurance like a Parris Island drill sergeant practicing his profession. At twelve, he had been seized by Cossacks and forced into a work gang. He had wandered the steppes of Russia for almost a year and a half, boy-turned-man before his time who knew that he had to keep a wary eye on the Cossacks mounted on horses alongside of him, whips at the ready as they sat high in the saddle. That year of forced labor haunts my brother and me with the same kind of isolation we have read about in frontier captivity narratives, where children must make their way through forested miles of haunted landscape. For our father, just one more test of endurance that his God had set in his path. "Had your Judaism been stronger," Kafka writes to his own father, "your example would have been more compelling." Kafka's father was no more like our father than his *Amerika* was like our America. Had Abe or I offered advice to our father, we would have urged him to pay less heed to God and more to the American imperatives his sons worshiped.

And yet, even with that burden of Europe, he made the journey away from home and into manhood. Only it was a journey from which he emerged in much the same condition as he went in, tattooed by the tribal history of the shtetl. There could be no doubt that he was man enough. But a man who would be of Europe forever, aged before his time. Years later, when I first read Isaac Babel, I actually thought that he must have known my father. Of course, he hadn't. The Jews of Babel's Odessa were less fearful as well as more sophisticated than that Galician peasantry to which my father belonged. Yet I still see him tramping through the Russian steppes, as if in an Eisenstein film, cold air permeating his longing for escape into a place that could offer him safety. The experience of being forcibly taken from his home must have been an extension of everything he knew about a Europe that was a knife to the throat of the shtetl. The baggage of the Cossacks would prove his baggage, too.

It was too much to hope that he not carry that baggage with him to America. Still, I like to think of him as he moves toward manhood. In the movie in my mind, I watch him struggle against the emptiness of the steppes, lost in the dead space as he wanders into a flat endless horizon. I think of him as a boy bold beyond his needs, like Benya Krik, Babel's Odessa gangster. I think of him pushing across a vast white blankness, one eye on the Cossacks, the other on an America already just beyond the horizon. In all the photographs of Babel that I have seen, he looks remarkably like the last picture that was taken of my father in Europe. I know how childish the fantasy is. Yet that God in whom my father believed so passionately can play the fool with any of us. Like Babel, my father understood why the joke is always on those who survive.

Among immigrant fathers, the obligations of sons were assumed. Among American sons, knowledge of how and for whom America worked was what defined a man. That knowledge, not the dead rituals of our father's Europe, was important to my brother and me. We both understand this to this day. Yet I still can't explain to Abe the reason why I was excused from *Neilah*, the last attempt to catch God's ear on Yom Kippur before he slammed shut the gates of judgment. In our father's eyes, his older son already had paid God's price—and with interest. Is my brother unable to understand that our father simply decided that God did not need me because even God had His limits? That I was crippled meant that I had earned a way out of any further obligation. That Abe was whole meant that he would stand with those whose job it was to beg God to be inscribed in the Book of Life.

Scorched by memory's fires, our imaginary argument continues. Abe tells me of how he asked our father why his presence,
not mine, was needed. Before the question can be framed, the answer is apparent. At least, to my brother it is. God's rage is not
for worship. I was granted immunity because, in our father's
eyes, God had overstepped His own boundaries when He created
the virus which took my legs. In such a spiritual free-fall, ritual
was just another bargaining chip between God and man.

My brother refuses to accept this. Not that he cannot understand it. There are certain immunities a man claims from fate
or accident or illness, but they are not to be granted as if they
carried lifelong tenure. An immunity gained so many years ago
is beyond even God's power to grant. My brother does not even
try to keep the irritation from his voice as we speak. We are beyond the dead father. "Because even devotion ends when there
is no justice. Do you think that just because you lose your legs,
obligation ends?" In our father's mind, the balance has been
struck. Losing my legs is enough. Not even the pious are beyond making their own corrupt bargains with the Lord of the
Universe.

In the lives of immigrant fathers, redemption took on the shape
of American sons. Our job was to make the world safe for him,
just as on grafittied schoolyard walls the intention is to distract
the mind from what is going on inside. Like the kiss of October's
crisp air or a single yellow tulip in the garden of the Episcopal
priest on the bottom of the hill on Rochambeau Avenue, ours
was a world in which order was to be the miracle that would be
served. A pear tree stood behind the synagogue, its ripe yellow
fruit tempting the strictures of Yom Kippur fasting. It is one of
the pictures held by American sons. My brother and I will each
run the risk of not believing, in defiance of our father and his

God. The immigrant father still imposes self and will on us, still *davens*, rocking on heel and toe, to praise that God in whom he believes with such simple passion that it is the one thing he possesses of which his American sons are afraid.

He was a pious man in a nation where even piety had to absorb the styles of Hollywood manhood. Think of Karl Malden playing the Catholic priest in *On the Waterfront*, crying, "Gimme a beer!" to show how regular a Joe he is. Think of Orson Welles in the role of Father Maple thundering against the darkness in John Huston's filming of *Moby Dick*. Like all American sons, my brother and I hungered for power and toughness. But we learned that human nature is not necessarily the nature of those American sons. Had it been his choice to make, our father would have come down on the side of the language of obedience for us, too. We envied his faith as well as his simplicity. Study. Learn. Pray. Be a wise man, a sage. With all the disappointment he must have felt in the triumph of America that he witnessed in the two of us, did he ever sense how much his sons would mourn that immigrant who fed us shame and love?

For immigrant fathers and American sons had such different ideas about what made a man a man. We each carried the ambitions of what we hoped to achieve. We each felt obligated to the self that existed in the mind's eye. Times change—and obligations, like debts, change with them. For our immigrant father, prayer had less to do with how man acknowledged God than with how God chose to acknowledge man. He *davened* into hope, gave himself over to it eagerly, wholeheartedly. For us, prayer was another false note reverberating through his European wilderness, chaining him to the past. What haunted us was the desire to be American men. And we wanted more than an immigrant father could provide in a nation that belonged to the sons, not to the fathers.

Yet as my brother and I wedged ourselves between father and country, we understood that he was lost in our America. The country simply possessed a very different idea of what a man was supposed to be than his own idea. His limited perspective on manhood was what we fled, as America's sons have been doing since Cotton Mather discovered that the true wilderness lay within the embattled heart. We staked our claim against his immigrant ethos. Both Abe and I felt doubt about the paths we had chosen. If our father's way is not better, he himself, we each sense, is.

The incidents are small, the talents fleeting. To look at the America that the immigrants sons chose to pursue, one invariably begins with the price demanded for their success. "This is no country for old men," wrote Yeats. He was not, of course, speaking of America but of what time invariably does to bodies as well as to dreams. Yet even if it was not his intention, Yeats might have been speaking for those American sons who lingered in the shadows of their immigrant fathers. Manhood as idea or image has little enough to do with the myths we were all raised on. However boyish and puerile those myths might be, one must say this much in their favor: they spoke of what legitimately could be asked of men in this country.

At the end of John Ford's *Stagecoach*, the boyish Ringo Kid rides off with his whore with a heart of gold. There is not much there for imagining manhood beyond John Wayne's awkward limitations as masculine icon. Yet the scene provides us with an effective contrast to what men in America worship today— power. The ability to impose one's bodily presence on others is now considered the only indispensable aspect of being a man. In business, in sports, in universities, even in domestic life, men are urged to celebrate how they can bully others into submission. A "real man" is meant to impose his will and power upon a hostile world. It is not enough that we hail those able to press their needs upon others. Never before in history, not even during the Gilded Age, has this nation been so open in its worship of wealth and power. We are quite willing to ignore those who behave with courage or integrity, since these are the qualities that make us uncomfortable. Like Jonah in the belly of the beast, we sense the sea heaving around our darkness. The wind howls us into silence, the waves lash against the beast's body. And my father's God remains intent on pinching us in the midst of our flight from all those obligations He wants us to assume. That men can make of necessity a virtue is among the oldest of cliches. Yet the one truly unforgivable sin a man can commit in today's America is to show that he is physically afraid. Other sins are easily forgiven. The cheat, the liar, the bully—each is excused by a nation which views manhood itself as a form of cheating, lying, and bullying. For a man to brag is considered poor taste only when bragging fails to match performance. Even young boys recognize the truth of Vince Lombardi's dictum, "Winning isn't everything; it's the only thing." Like underwear, morality changes. But losing alone places a man beyond redemption.

American sons learn to worship not strength of character nor the ability to endure hardship in the pursuit of some larger interest. Ours is a nation content to worship the purity of power and the imposition of force. Not by accident has football surpassed baseball in the affections of American men. Football can speak directly to our love of power. The appeal of the game is that it is open about the ways the nation rewards bullying. Its essence is how one team can impose itself on the other team. It is probably also not by accident that in no other game is the word "courage" bruited about so frequently. Exaggerated obligations of success and purpose frame the game of football, just as they increasingly reflect our moments as men.

I sit on the stone steps of the small apartment building in which my brother and I live with our parents. In the street where I once slashed a hockey stick into the empty air, trying to savage the black puck across the manhole cover, Abe is playing a game of touch football with a group of his friends. I watch as their obligations unfold, filled with an envy as sharp as the press of this November cold. Abe is thirteen, I am seventeen, and the late October air is crisp with the anticipation of winter. My brother and the two other boys on his side clap their hands in that imitation enthusiasm so common with adolescents. In cadence, I hear their voices drone in unison. Childish rhythm of "One Mississippi, two Mississippi." The shape of grievance on a cold afternoon. My brother spins, runs in the direction of the manhole cover to my left. I see the tight spiral cut the air as Abe's body sails high, hands straining outward, until his fingers close on the football and he comes crashing down to creosote, wincing as he hits the ground. But he holds the ball. A moment that leaves me pleased—but burning with envy.

Years later, when Abe is a graduate student at Duke, his wrist aches and he has it x-rayed, only to discover that he broke it when he dove through the air and caught that football. A minor blip in a man's life, a twinge of pain to signal a change in the weather. At a writer's conference in Arkansas in the spring of 1996, I meet an artist who used to play touch football with Abe at the University of Memphis, where they both were teaching. American rituals. The Art Department against the History Department in touch football. He speaks admiringly of Abe's pass-catching ability, and when I mention this to my brother in a real telephone conversation, I hear him laugh happily. In the lives of American sons, the dues of adolescence pay for the passage through. It is not something immigrant fathers could understand. It is not like wandering the Russian steppes. My father was almost the exact age his son, my brother, was when he crashed against asphalt and broke his wrist. My brother knows that a wrist that aches when it rains is a small price to pay for a moment that commands a man's memory of his body. The ache will always be as rich in memory as it is dull as pain.

It's easy enough to ridicule such coming-of-age rites. Stale ideas and dead attitudes, our masculine imperatives have led to the rhetorical nonsense of the men's movement. Yet it is difficult to survive without certain stale ideas and dead attitudes, particularly in an age in which gender consciousness rises to a flood. Like hawks surveying possibility, the sexes eye each other. Consciousness of gender has a lot to say about men and women, and very little to say about what manhood is. Even as a word, "manhood" leaves us in a sweat. Constructed or deconstructed, it is a linguistic irritation that scratches at the mind like a bad case of psoriasis. In a parody of the past, Bly's Iron John tells his ghost stories around the camp fires of feverish imaginations. And that, we are told, is what manhood is.

And yet, American sons should not be shamed out of manhood. If there is too much nostalgia about the thing, that doesn't make it less necessary or less real. Like the prospect of a grand affair, manhood can be both a sleazy interlude or a true passion. That it partakes of both as it hammers us into the shapes that form us should be obvious. But it isn't. For an immigrant father, the quest was for that God whom he feared in the depths of his heart even as he wandered across the frozen steppes, aware of the immense horizon that lay beyond that prison house called Russia. For a brother whose rage still resounds in my imagination, the need was that I finally admit what he had been called upon to pay so that I could total up the debts and obligations that were rightfully mine. And for me, the truth was the admission that I am more accurate than I know when I speak of disease as a sharing.

Brother and son, I stand in the mind's storm, as much a stranger to those I love as they are to me. It's not enough to accept a brother's anger, to understand his rage at having to stand in for me. It's not enough to search for that immigrant father, alone in a hostile world, as he maneuvers through the blank immensities of landscape, his faith frozen to his fear as he prepares for passage to an America that exists only in his mind. I will never know whether I am as good a man as my brother or as our father. I will never know if my endurance matches or is less than theirs. I only know that as I close in on my life, still trying to balance it out, it is the need to stand as a man that I have come to value. More and more, that has emerged as the thing itself, the portrait revealed, where I see myself—brother, son, father, stranger.

DATE DUE

DE 13 '02			
GAYLORD			PRINTED IN U.S.A